THE
COLLECTED VERSE OF
ROBERT HILLYER

D1455448

THE

COLLECTED VERSE

OF

ROBERT HILLYER

ALFRED · A · KNOPF

NEW YORK

1933

245315

PS
329
H65 A6
COPY 3

FIRST EDITION

Copyright 1933 by Robert Hillyer

All rights reserved. No part of this book may be reproduced in any form without permission in writing from the publisher, except by a reviewer who may quote brief passages in a review to be printed in a magazine or newspaper.

Manufactured in the United States of America

GIFT

TO

DOROTHY HANCOCK HILLYER
and
STANLEY HANCOCK HILLYER

ACKNOWLEDGMENT

The poems in this volume originally appeared in the following periodicals: The Adelphi, The American Caravan, The Atlantic Monthly, The Bookman (New York), The Bookman (London), Books, The Dial, The Forum, Harper's, The Harvard Advocate, The Harvard Monthly, The Hound and Horn, The Independent, The London Mercury, The Lyric, The Nation, The New Republic, The New Adelphi, The New English Weekly, The Outlook, Poetry: A Magazine of Verse, The Reviewer, The Seven Arts, Smoke; and in the following volumes: Sonnets and Other Lyrics (Harvard University Press, 1917); The Five Books of Youth (Brentano, 1920); The Hills Give Promise (B. J. Brimmer, 1922); The Halt in the Garden (Elkin Mathews, 1925); The Seventh Hill (Viking Press, 1928); The Gates of the Compass (Viking Press, 1930).

To the editors and publishers concerned, grateful acknowledgment is made for permission to reprint the poems in this book.

I should also like to thank the friends, too numerous for specific mention, who have so generously helped me in the past and in the preparation of this present volume with their criticism, both favourable and adverse. And to Miss Dorothy Viets I owe deep gratitude for her long and helpful co-operation in the arranging of the manuscript.

R. S. H.

CONTENTS

SHORTER POEMS

CONTENTS

CONTENTS

SHORTER POEMS

For Ever

When I say For Ever I think of the temple of Zeus,
The broken drums of the columns buried in grass;
Marble avails not, words are of little use,
It is longer than miles from Olympia to Patras.

For Ever is marble, For Ever is white and tall,
But the road I follow ends in a tangle of weeds
Where lie the drums of the columns, the stones of the wall,
Broken letters of a word that no man reads.

Remote

The farthest country is Tierra del Fuego,
That is the bleakest and the loneliest land;
There are the echoing mountains of felspar,
And salt winds walking the empty sand.

This country remembers the birth of the moon
From a rocky rib of the young earth's side;
It heard the white-hot mountains bellow
Against the march of the first flood tide.

I lifted a shell by the glass-green breakers
And heard what no man has heard before,
The whisper of steam in the hot fern forest
And slow feet crunching the ocean floor.

I saw the slanted flash of a seagull
When a sheaf of light poured over the clouds,
I heard the wind in the stiff dune grasses,
But I saw no sail and I heard no shrouds.

To a promontory of Tierra del Fuego
I climbed at noon and stretched my hand
Toward another country, remoter and bleaker.

Never Fear

Never fear the phantom bird
Meditating in the Fens;
Night will come and quench your eyes,
Blind at last like other men's;
Never fear the tales you heard
In the rhetoric of lies.

Nothing here will challenge you,
Not the heron, tall and white,
Countersign upon the edge
Of the waterfall of night.
This is Avilon's canoe,
Eden murmurs in the sedge.

Here! my hand in pledge of rest.
Drift at random, all is well.
Twilight is a slow lagoon,
Dark will be a citadel.
Travellers who know the west
But report the waning moon.

In the citadel of peace
Hang the trophies of the world,
Yet no barons don their mail,

And no pennant is unfurled.
Daily robe, the Golden Fleece,
Daily cup, the Holy Grail.

The Garden on the Moors

The Swordsman of the Quiet Gate
Is pacing at his wonted post,
Wherefore no wind can agitate
The pond that holds the lily's ghost;
Wherefore the fountain flashing high
Its spear of fire against the sky,
The green pavilion and its host
Assured to us until we die.

When we would sleep, we turn away
Sure of reunion after sleep,
Knowing the crystal slopes of day
Await the shepherds and their sheep.
We hold in store our last embrace
For our awaking in this place,
Sure of the vigil One will keep
Whose voice we know not, nor his face.

If for an instant he should drowse
And sleep should put his dream to flight,
Our leaves would scatter from the boughs,
Our garden wither in the blight;
The sphere of happiness we share
Float up the morning's winding stair,

To burst, a bubble of delight,
Casting its colours down the air.

The reason for his patient guard
We cannot guess; we only know
The roadway is austere and hard
Where his mild feet go to and fro.
We only know that where we are
We need no earthly calendar,
But drift with shining hours that flow
From star to sun and sun to star.

In the Tidal Marshes

White above the afterflare
The moon rides up the brimming air
Singing in minor key the theme
Of light as music in a dream.
Lovers lying on the dune
Turn from each other toward the moon
And feel a tide far mightier
Than mortal love mount up to her
Who drowns in her magnetic flood
Mere urgencies of flesh and blood.
This is the hour the dying pass
Without a sigh to mist the glass,
So gently the translation made
From shadows to the world of shade.
So one who walks alone will stand
With love and death on either hand,
Invisible companions, who
Though cunningly disguised as two
Yet in reality are one,
Love the flesh, and death the bone.
He walks and feels the spectres glide
Along with him on either side,
And closer draws, to ward them off,
His cloak of loneliness, the stuff

Of pride, the pattern of control,
To hold them from his naked soul.
The long boardwalk lies dim before
Across the salt marsh to the shore.
My brother Sea, how tide on tide
Your waters shift, while you abide;
From wave on wave, lost in each other,
Your undiminished voice, my brother.
My sister Moon, how ray on ray
Is woven your unearthly day;
From ever changing gleam and glister
Your constancy of light, my sister.
My father God, how thought on thought
Your undiscovered mind is wrought;
From love whose end is death you gather
Your everlastingness, my father.
This is the hour the heart discovers
How love is mightier than lovers,
And this the hour the dying pass
Through death and know not what it was.
And one shall stand upon the shore
And he shall ponder them no more,
But dive into the sea, and swim
Far out, and peace shall go with him.

Black Magic

Three friends of mine who know my heart,
I have decreed your death today;
And through what means, and by what art,
Who but yourselves could ever say?
I could not suffer you to part
Flinging my secrets on your way.

Who knows through what impetuous word
My lore escapes your careless lips,
Through what small syllable, the bird
That was my golden captive slips
And sings to those who having heard
Will slay it with envenomed quips?

That King of Knossos who would build
A Labyrinth around his thought
Sagaciously and justly willed
Death to the architects who wrought;
And thus the winged word was stilled
Which once set free is never caught.

Friends whom I love, for fear I might
Have cause to love you less, I stir
Three melting forms of wax, and light

Three tapers for three friends that were,
Till three slim phantoms take their flight
Between the whorls of smoking myrrh.

Spiritism

This pathway marked No Thoroughfare
Is obviously barred,
But vulgar people love to stare
In someone else's yard.

It is not reverent but rude
To spy beyond the bounds
Like raw plebeians who intrude
Upon patrician grounds

And bribe the servants to undo
The door a little crack —
A burglar's glimpse, a keyhole view,
Behind the Master's back.

A scandal, so it seems to me,
The way they force the doors
To trespass on the privacy
Of their superiors.

How much more fitting to await
The summons to attend,
Ride proudly through the open gate
And enter as a friend.

Masquerade

The curtains draw across the brain
And in that lighted house of mirth,
Secure from all the eyes of earth,
Our troupe of dreams come out again.

Folly has donned the sage's mask,
Wisdom appears the Knave of Hearts,
Yet in these topsy-turvy parts
They seem as real as one could ask;

As real as when they change their rôles
To be themselves and haunt the dream
Where for some hours of day they seem
Important to our sleeping souls.

Lullaby

The long canoe
Toward the shadowy shore,
One . . . two . . .
Three . . . four . . .
The paddle dips,
Turns in the wake,
Pauses, then
Forward again.
Water drips
From the blade to the lake.
Nothing but that,
No sound of wings;
The owl and bat
Are velvet things.
No wind awakes,
No fishes leap,
No rabbits creep
Among the brakes.
The long canoe
At the shadowy shore,
One . . . two . . .
Three . . . four . . .
A murmur now
Under the prow

Where rushes bow
To let us through.
One . . . two . . .
Upon the shore,
Three . . . four . . .
Upon the lake,
No one's awake,
No one's awake,
One . . . two . . .
No one, not even you.

Illuminated Manuscript

Happy art thou, my phantom saint,
As the quill draws out the whorls of paint
And the letter blossoms into a rose;
Word by word the slow book grows.

Out of the window I see the stream
Cleave the hill with a broken gleam.
The autumn sunset burns to a scar
And the sky is healed with a single star.

Around thee the pools of shadow blend,
Fingers loosen and labours end.
The ink has dried on the supple quill
And sunset burned out over the hill.

Thou hast left thy work, O my phantom saint,
Unfinished, but not one letter faint.
The spirit blossoms into a rose,
And word by word the slow book grows.

Dead Man's Corner

Here is the crossroads where the slain
Were piled so deep we could not pass.
Now dreams alone renew the stain
Of blood long soaked into the grass.

If ambulance to save the maimed
Or gunwagon to maim the sound,
Both must proceed, while rightly named
The Mort Homme darkens all the ground.

As long ago wheels took the groove
In necessary roads again,
Crunching the bones that could not move
To move the limbs of living men;

With cracked and beaten lips that taste
Commands like acid but obeyed,
We still with leaden nightmare haste
Convey our shadows through the shade.

War is a most forgotten fear
But peace will not be out of mind.
We drive our ambulances here
God help us! and the road is blind.

When the Heart Cracks

When the heart cracks
There is nothing to do about it
And that nothing means the cracking of the mind.
When mind and heart crack
There is nothing to do about it
But set the spirit free.
Spirit can not crack
It can rise from the carnal tree
And soar, — whither?
That much we can not know.
But when heart and mind crack
Spirit must go
To nothingness perhaps?
Perhaps to another tree?
But certainly it must be set free.

XXth Century

There is no time,
No time,
There is no time,
Not even for a kiss,
Not even for this,
Not even for this rhyme.

It is May
And blossoms sway
In sifted snow
Under the moon.
I only know
That I can not stay,
For today is May
And tomorrow June.

An arrow shot
From an idiot's bow,
That is my lot
And I must go.

There is no time,
No time,
There is no time,

Not even for a kiss,
Not even for this,
Not even for this rhyme, —
   No . . . !

Folk Song

The stars came, but her Love came never,
And standing there on the bank of the river,
" Come back! " she said to the waves of the river,
But they hurried away and they came back never.
" You come not back to the land of my lover,"
She said to the hurrying waves of the river,
" Then will I go with you, waves of the river,
To oceans far from the land of my lover."
Under the starlight the girl and the river
Hurry away and they come back never.

Folk Song

Now time has gathered to itself
    The lily and the rose,
To mould upon a dusty shelf
    Where no man knows.

Now all things lovely fail and wane,
    The tender petals close,
And in the dawn shall bloom again
    No lily, no rose.

Now from the garden of your face
    The lily and the rose
Are gathered to a dusty place
    Where no man knows.

Folk Song

O Mariners of the Sun, you have reached your port!
Under the Mountain of Twilight how still the mooring!
The golden boat grows dim, and you disembark.
In the taverns of nether earth may you meet rare sport,
And loves madder than ours if no more enduring,
And a night sweeter than our night though as short.
O Mariners, in that city of the dark
Forget not the greetings I gave you for my friend:
Tell her how sometimes I would rush out to find her,
And sometimes I bide unmoved, but for ever send
Love, and for ever love. And again remind her
That soon or late I will join her in the end.

Spinning Song

" Never think of me, never remember,"
She was singing in her chamber
High in the attic under the eaves
Where dusty windows are screened with leaves.

"Never think of me, never remember,"
She was singing in her chamber,
She did not hear the knocker clang
Or a voice below that also sang.

Her wheel whirred on, the flax spun out
A cobweb strand as thin as doubt,
The green leaves tapped on the window pane,
And someone knocked and knocked again.

She did not hear the knocker clang
Or the voice below that also sang:
"Not many years — and the heart still young
Weaves new words for the willing tongue.

" Not many years have passed, and the heart
Still young is led to where thou art
By a slender strand of flaxen hair,
By a strand of song as thin as air."

The wheel whirred on, and grain by grain
The grey dust filmed the window pane;
She did not hear him when he knocked
For the leaves were thick and the windows locked.

She did not hear, now faint and far
Like music heard through doors ajar:
" Not many years have passed, are past,
But dust will stifle the heart at last."

High in the attic under the eaves
The dusty windows are screened with leaves.
" Never think of me, never remember,"
She was singing in her chamber.

And When the Prince Came

May the castle lie in slumber
For another thousand years,
Beldame fallen by her spindle,
Sentries full-length by their spears.
Sleeping hands no toil shall cumber,
Sleeping hearts no love shall kindle,
Sleeping eyes are void of tears.

May the blue flame in the hallways
Burn like tapers by the dead,
May no clarion of duty
Rouse the old King from his bed.
And the Princess, may she always
Lie in peace, for Sleeping Beauty
Blossoms only to be shed.

In my vision I had bound her
To my fate, a mortal wife
Wakened from a sleep immortal
By the urgent kiss of life.
But I left her as I found her
And above the southern portal
This I lettered with my knife:

27

" Loves there are that feast in giving;
Slumber still — my love was such;
Bonds that strengthen as they sever,
Lips that pause and will not touch.
Sleep, Beloved, safe from living;
Sleep, Beloved, safe for ever
From the one who loved too much."

Epitaph

Here by this quiet pool,
Under the quiet sun,
   Constance remembers
How rose the beautiful
Lord from oblivion,
   Flame from the embers.

She dreams in light among
Legions of mortals whom
   Darkness convinces;
Dreams, till she hear the young
Prince by her lonely tomb
   Calling his Princess.

Elegy

On a Dead Mermaid Washed Ashore
at Plymouth Rock

Pallidly sleeping, the Ocean's mysterious daughter
Lies in the lee of the boulder that shattered her charms.
Dawn rushes over the level horizon of water
And touches to flickering crimson her face and her arms,
While every scale in that marvelous tail
Quivers with colour like sun on a Mediterranean sail.

Could you not keep to the ocean that lulls the equator,
Soulless, immortal, and fatally fair to the gaze?
Or were you called to the North by an ecstasy greater
Than any you knew in those ancient and terrible days
When all your delight was to flash on the sight
Of the wondering sailor and lure him to death in the watery
night?

Was there, perhaps, on the deck of some far-away vessel
A lad from New England whose fancy you failed to
ensnare?
Who, born of this virtuous rock, and accustomed to wrestle
With beauty in all of its forms, became your despair,

And awoke in your breast a mortal unrest
That dragged you away from the south to your death in the
    cold northwest?

Pallidly sleeping, your body is shorn of its magic,
But Death gives a soul to whatever is lovely and dies.
Now Ocean reclaims you again, lest a marvel so tragic
Remain to be mocked by our earthly and virtuous eyes,
And reason redeems already what seems
Only a fable like all our strange and beautiful dreams.

Scherzo

The flower-girl, singing, comes up from the river,
Up through the field to the street of the village,
Bringing her basket heaped high with the pillage
Of riverside violet, lily, and rush.
The rays of the morning flicker and quiver
Warm on her arms and her glistening face,
And twinkle on anklets that jangle together
With tinkle of bells and melodious jingle
As gay as a robin and clear as a thrush.

The wind is awake with her, fingering ribbons and lace
That flutter in tatters, bright like a paradise feather;
The wind is awake with her up from the river so early
With songs that are part of the sunrise and mingle
With the singing of birds in the willow.

The herdboy has lifted his curly head from the pillow
Of grass at her singing;
And bows to her mockingly, makes a grimace,
And laughs to the laughter that ripples her face
Till the hillside is ringing.

Wind, wind, all night through the Emperor's gardens
You gathered the weary delight of the wise and the witty

And perfume that curled out of urns of gold.
Wind, all night through the city
You gathered the word that murders, the whisper that
    hardens
The minds of men in a horrible mould.

Scatter the cargo you gathered, and blow through the hair
Of the flower-girl singing at dawn through the street;
Scatter the cargo you gathered, and bear
The silvery laughter that rings from the hill.

I have opened my window. Pour over me; spill
All the spring at my feet!

For Maister Geoffrey Chaucer

A bard there was, and that a worthy wight,
Who, from the time that he began to write,
Served God and beauty with an humble mind,
And most of all he knew and loved mankind.
Laughing he was, and quick at many a jest,
The Lord loves mirth, — the devil take the rest!
A simple grace ere wine be poured at dinner,
A ready hand outstretched to saint and sinner,
A prayer at times, not lengthy but devout,
This was our poet's faith without a doubt.
Travel he loved, and wonders had to tell
Of royal France and Italy as well,
And everywhere he went, his furtive pen
Took down the secrets of his fellow men,
Their faces and their stories, high and low,
From lordly Petrarch and Boccaccio
Unto the meanest villein who could hold
A tavern audience with the tales he told.
But with his scrivening, he never swerved
From duty to King Edward whom he served,
And though he roamed both France and Italy,
England was where he always longed to be,
And thither he returned with magic spoils
That England might have pleasure of his toils,

And hear his brave, chivalric stories sung
By English pilgrims in the English tongue.
Noble his spirit was, and gay his heart.
A judge of wine, a master of his art,
He loved all men, nor was ashamed to show it;
He was a very parfit gentil poet,
Gentil in life and parfit in his rhyme, —
God send us such another in our time!

A Failure

Evening has come, young man;
What have you done today?

I have fashioned a younger man
Out of the ageless clay.
He will pass invisible
Through crowds in the market square;
They will say, " Did you hear a bell? "
They will say, " How queer to smell
Incense in open air! "
Wherever he plants his feet,
Wherever he skims his heel,
The air will go mad and sweet,
The asphalt will skirl and reel.
They will say, " We can hear the beat
Of a mighty revolving wheel
In a powerhouse far off."

Young man, that is not enough.

On the Boulevard

Two old men walked together down the street,
Two late survivors of atrocious years,
Comparing memories of sharp deceit,
And crimes wherein they were the pioneers.

A child ran by the cronies, and looked back.
They turned to one another then, and smiled,
Smudging her whiteness with imagined black,
And whispering cynic futures for the child.

Seven score years grinned shamelessly at five.
Half wondering, half shy, she turned again,
Thinking that if her father were alive
He'd be just like those kind old gentlemen.

Reunion

Now welcome back, and health! he said.
After so many years apart
I thought that half of us were dead
And half in wheel chairs or deranged.
Sit down! We all have lots to tell;
It warms the cockles of my heart
To see how little you have changed. . . .
The clock ticked on. *Farewell, farewell.*

Here's whiskey, John; here's brandy, Ned;
What's yours, old man? I'm glad to see
There's not one grey hair on your head; —
Why, hang it! you look twenty-five.
The world's your oyster; I'm the shell,
But at this moment I should be
Thankful I'm even still alive. . . .
Farewell. The clock ticked on. *Farewell.*

There's Bill and Toby over there
Just as they used to be, he said.
They'll wrangle all the night, that pair,
After so many years apart.
Fill up, — lots more when this is gone;

Don't sit there staring like the dead.
Good God! Something is at my heart. . . .
Farewell, farewell. The clock ticked on.

Ageing Coquette

The rusty sawing in the grass
    Goes with the autumn in the air,
And now the dame before her glass
    Weeps at her wisps of hair.

She, so aghast at katydids,
    Will shriek to see the flakes of snow,
While frantically she tears the lids
    Off rouge-pots in a row.

Vanity is a little sin
    But tedious; — if she will not doff
That lamentable, worn-out skin,
    Then, Winter, *blow* it off!

The Tryst

Neither spoke; the silence clung,
They were old that had been young.

Through notched hills the moonlight came;
Two lights plumbed the dark below;
Everything was just the same,
Even the quiet silver glow
On the shingle roofs like snow; —
But a stranger bore her name.

Here where young desire was mated
To the memory of a face;
Where long vigil desolated
Every beauty of the place,
Came at last the hour of grace,
But not he, the long-awaited.

There they stood, and there they slew
Each the hope the other nourished.
Ghosts of flesh and blood, they drew
Shadowy life from shades that perished,
And the dreams that they had cherished
Seemed the stranger, now they knew.

Neither spoke; the silence clung.
They were old that had been young.

Saint Sylvius

Ever he loved the wood and field,
The water rushing through the weir,
And so he dropped his knightly shield
And flung away his spear.

He turned from battle and from quest,
From heavenly Grail and earthly feast,
Became the woodland's welcome guest,
The friend of every beast.

And often would he sit and fish
With bait but not a single hook;
No trout lay ever on his dish, —
They fattened in the brook.

And often would he chase the deer,
But seeing none upon the hill
Find twenty browsing without fear
Beside his own doorsill.

He even loved the wicked snake,
Explaining lamely that the devil
Should be well nourished for the sake
Of Him who conquers evil.

Happy he lived with bird and beast,
Well known and well beloved of both.
Two fears alone perturbed his breast:
Death and the sin of sloth.

And still he never fails to wince
At thought of death or mortal taint, —
Not knowing that he died long since,
Or that he is a saint.

Moo!

Summer is over, the old cow said,
And they'll shut me up in a draughty shed
To milk me by lamplight in the cold,
But I won't give much for I am old.
It's long ago that I came here
Gay and slim as a woodland deer;
It's long ago that I heard the roar
Of Smith's white bull by the sycamore.
And now there are bones where my flesh should be;
My backbone sags like an old roof tree,
And an apple snatched in a moment's frolic
Is just so many days of colic.
I'm neither a Jersey nor Holstein now
But only a faded sort of cow.
My calves are veal and I had as lief
That I could lay me down as beef;
Somehow, they always kill by halves, —
Why not take me when they take my calves?
Birch turns yellow and sumac red,
I've seen this all before, she said,
I'm tired of the field and tired of the shed.
There's no more grass, there's no more clover;
Summer is over, summer is over.

Seven Epigrams

I

Be calm, O soul so often tried,
Sleep once was thine, and sleep shall come again,
Ere thou wert born, when thou hast died,
   Not thine the pain.

Before thou wokest from the womb
Sorrow and hate were old, and fear and need,
Thou didst not know them; in the tomb
   Thou shalt not heed.

Serenely face thine undertaking.
Sorrow is great? thy slumber shall be deep,
And life nought but a moment's waking
   From sleep to sleep.

II

The sunset takes up half the land,
The dark the other half,
And in the dusk between I stand
Leaning upon my staff.

The shade commands me to lament,
The sunlight to rejoice;
Then night usurps the continent
And nullifies the choice.

III

I wearied of disaster:
I swore to murder Fate,
And make myself the master
Of my terrene estate.

I slew my foe, and gaily
Supplanted him I slew,
And do more damage daily
Than Fate could ever do.

IV

The thinkers light their lamps in rows
    From street to street, and then
The night creeps up behind, and blows
    Them quickly out again.

While age limps groping toward his home,
    Hearing the feet of youth
From dark to dark that sadly roam
    The suburbs of the Truth.

V

A smile will turn away green eyes
That laughter could not touch,
The dangers of those subtleties,
The stealthy, clever hand,
Should not affright you overmuch
If you but understand
How Judas, clad in Oxford grey,
Could walk abroad on Easter Day.

VI

I see that Hermes unawares,
Has left his footprints on the path;
See here, he fell, and in his wrath
He pulled out several golden hairs
Among the brambles. Guard them well,
The hairs of gods are valuable.

VII

Bring hemlock, black as Cretan cheese,
And mix a sacramental brew;
A worthy drink for Socrates,
Why not for you?

Ballade

The dull-eyed girl in bronze implores Apollo
To warm these dying satyrs and to raise
Their withered wreaths that rot in every hollow
Or smoulder redly in the pungent haze.
The shining reapers, gone these many days,
Have left their fields disconsolate and sear,
Like bony sand uncovered to the gaze,
In this, the ebb-tide of the year.

My wisest comrade turns into a swallow
And flashes southward as the thickets blaze
In awful splendour; I, who can not follow,
Confront the skies' unmitigated greys.
The cynic faun whom I have known betrays
A dangerous mood at night, and seems austere
Beneath the autumn noon's distempered rays,
In this, the ebb-tide of the year.

Ice quenches all reflection in the shallow
Lagoon whose trampled margin still displays
Upheaval where the centaurs used to wallow;
And where my favourite unicorns would graze,
A few wild ducks scream lamentable lays
Of shrill derision desperate with fear,

Bleak note on note, phrase on discordant phrase,
In this, the ebb-tide of the year.

Poor girl, how soon our garden world decays,
Our metals tarnish, our loves disappear;
Dull-eyed we haunt these unfrequented ways,
In this, the ebb-tide of the year.

Nocturne

Chords, tremendous chords,
    Over the stricken plain.
The night is calling her ancient lords
    Back to their own again.

Vast, unhappy song,
    From incalculable space,
Calling the heavy-browed, the strong,
    Out of their resting-place.

Far from the lighted town,
    Over the snow and ice,
Their dreadful feet go up and down
    Seeking a sacrifice.

And can you find a way
    Where They will not come after?
The vast chords hesitate and sway
    Into a sudden laughter.

Nocturne

There was a fountain in the court
That played all night,
But the night was short,
And the morning grey.
There was a whip-poor-will that sang
In the wan moonlight,
And music sprang
From the shattered spray.
I lay in the grass and touched your hand;
You drew it away.
You understand
The flames that start from the touch of a hand,
And you drew it away;
And desire froze at the sorry part
I was forced to play,
And fear like a north wind fanned
My tropic heart,
Lest you arise and fly me.
I held my breath and heard
Moth wings whir by me,
I heard a petal fall by the garden wall,
And a dreaming bird
Stir in imagined flight.

There was a fountain in the court
That played all night, —
But the night was short.

Nocturne

If the deep wood is haunted, it is I
Who am the ghost; not the tall trees
Nor the white moonlight slanting down like rain,
Filling the hollows with bright pools of silver.

A long train whistle serpentines around the hill
Now shrill, now far away.
Tell me, from what dark smoky terminal
What train sets out for yesterday?

Or, since our spirits take off and resume
Their flesh as travellers their cloaks, O tell me where,
In what age and what country you will come,
That I may meet you there.

Nocturne

I felt the wind on my cheek
And I awoke.
The night had come.
Out of the dark, spoke
The flowing creek, —
All else was dumb.

My clothes were wet with dew,
My hands were caked with mud,
But the thought of you
Was a brazier to my blood.
And groping home
Through walls of black
I sang, " O never come,
Never come back! "

So long estranged, and now
So eloquently near
In the wind fanning my brow,
In the water singing clear,
Even in the vast black
And the valley lying dumb, —

O never come,
Never come back!

58

Thirty Pastorals

I

Ponder the tone; the broken theme
Sounds once for us, and not for long.
It is easy to forget a dream
However exquisite it seem,
It is easy to forget a song.

The Master does but improvise,
The final music is not yet;
But when it shakes eternal skies
I would not have you quite forget
The music of the mortal dream
We shared in joy, though not for long.
Ponder the tone, the broken theme,
It is easy to forget a song.

II

Piping Anne and husky Paul
Once they swelled our madrigal,
She watched him and he watched her,
Always out of tune they were.
Yet from two discords may be
Love's most tuneful harmony;
Such a music they have wrought,
        (they have wrought)
As to set our skill at naught.

Let the nightingale in vain
Lift his amorous refrain,
Let the dying reedy swan
Cease her prothalamion.
They are sunk in such a bliss
Deep as old Atlantic is.
End our song and come away
        (come away)
Music hath no more to say.

III

Full length on the hills of heaven
Daphnis lay at half past seven;
Heaven indeed it was to share
Morning with so loved, so fair,
As the one beside him there.

Quarter before eight, a sorry
Daphnis dwelt in Purgatory,
Too undone to think or say
How a morning of mid-May
Had become the Judgment Day.

Eight o'clock, and Daphnis made his
Penitential way to Hades,
Pricked with all the fiery spears
Of his own accusing fears
And the memory of her tears.

So in half an hour returning
From his bliss and from his burning,
Nothing left to lose or win;
Daphnis thought he'd best begin
To be born again in sin.

IV

Spring, put on your golden sandals,
Stride across the waning day,
Then at twilight chase the vandals
From our ruined world away.
Clear our heaven where the seven
Constellations watch and pray.

Melt the icy heart of winter,
Soothe the forest, tempest-tossed.
Though the shafts of moonlight splinter
On the crystals of the frost,
Make earth tingle with a single
Dream from all that she has lost.

Shod in beauty, swift newcomer,
Touch me also with your wand,
That I may divine the summer
In the first tight-folded frond,
From one tender hint, the splendour
Of the garden just beyond.

V

So ghostly then the girl came in
I never saw the turnstile twist
Down where the orchard trees begin
Lost in a reverie of mist.

And in the windless hour between
The last of daylight and the night,
When fields give up their ebbing green
And two bats interweave their flight,

I saw the turnstile glimmer pale
Just where the orchard trees begin,
But watching was of no avail,
Invisibly the girl came in.

I took one deep breath of the air
And lifted up my heavy heart;
It was not I who trembled there
But my immortal counterpart.

I knew that she had come again
Up from the orchard through the stile,
Without a sign to tell me when,
Though I was watching all the while.

VI

I watched the pond without lifting my eyes;
Shadow of leaves on shadow skies;
Scarves of colour twining through haze
And a bright bird flying with wings ablaze;
A bird flying over, the day in flight,
And I watched him pass without lifting my eyes.
It was enough, the shadow of delight,
The shadow of a bird over shadow skies.

The first white star unbound her hair;
The water trembled and she was there
Setting her foot on the darkening mirror
While round her the trees of night leaned nearer;
They gathering dark, she gathering light,
And I watched the pond without lifting my eyes;
It was enough, the shadow of night,
The shadow of a star in the shadow skies.

VII

The fireflies wink and glow,
The night is on the march,
The cricket clacks his castanets
And the moon hangs in the larch.
I will take my violin
And a few themes I will play:
Pizzicati for the fireflies,
Harmonics for the moonlight,
And a chord for the smell of hay.

I will play but a few bars,
And when the moon has set
I will listen to the stars.

VIII

It is the time of mooring now;
The pebbles scrape and the reeds are parted
Before the languid push of the prow.

It is the time of mooring now,
And where all day the swallow has darted
Dipping his wings in the sunny waves,
There is only a smooth, dark mirror spread
Where the dancers of the mist will tread.
The air is cool as the breath of caves,
And damp as the breath of steaming loam. . . .

It is the time of mooring now,
Ship your oars and come back home.

IX

Against my wall the summer weaves
Profundities of dusky leaves,
And many-petaled stars full-blown
In constellated whiteness sown;
I meditate with lazy eyes
My small estate in Paradise,
And very comforting to me
Is this familiarity.

X

When noon is blazing on the town,
The fields are loud with droning flies,
The people pull their curtains down,
And all the houses shut their eyes.

The palm leaf drops from your mother's hand
And she dozes there in a darkened room,
Outside there is silence on the land,
And only poppies dare to bloom.

Open the door and steal away
Through grain and briar shoulder high,
There are secrets hid in the heart of day,
In the hush and slumber of July.

Your face will burn a fiery red,
Your feet will drag through dusty flame,
Your brain turn molten in your head,
And you will wish you never came.

O never mind, go on, go on, —
There is a brook where willows lean;
To weave deep caverns from the sun,
And there the grass grows cool and green.

68

And there is one as cool as grass,
Lying beneath the willow tree,
Counting the dragon flies that pass,
And talking to the bumble bee.

She has not stirred since morning came,
She does not know how in the town
The earth shakes dizzily with flame,
And all the curtains are drawn down.

Sit down beside her; she can tell
The strangest secrets you would hear,
And cool as water in a well,
Her words flow down upon your ear. . . .

She speaks no more, but in your hair
Her fingers soft as lullabies
Fold up your senses unaware,
Into a poppy paradise.

And when you wake, the evening mist
Is rising up to float the hill,
And you will say, " The mouth I kissed,
The voice I heard . . . a dream . . . but still

" The grass is matted where she lay,
I feel her fingers in my hair " . . .
But your lamp is bright across the way,
And your mother knits in the rocking chair.

XI

August afternoon in a drowse,
No leaf moving on the boughs,
No ripple moving on the pool
Nor a thought in the mind of summer's fool
Who treads the shadow of delight;
Morning, afternoon, and night,
He treads the shadow of delight.

Tell him how the blackbirds flew
To form their flocks, two by two;
Warn him with the goldenrod
And brown seeds from the lily pod.
Stir the air with solemn warning
Afternoon and night and morning,
Till he heed your autumn warning.

Summer's fool will never heed
Though the whole earth go to seed.
Death will catch him unaware
With the vine leaves in his hair.
Leave him to his dream, for soon
Morning, night, or afternoon,
He will waken — all too soon!

XII

A month too late one firefly
    Cruises the night alone,
Strayed from the meadows of July
    Beneath an August moon.

Slowly above the sleeping phlox
    It mounts the rungs of air,
Until the cloudy moonlight mocks
    The solitary flare.

A starboard light far out at sea,
    A lantern on the fens,
Are lonely, but this lamp to me
    Is lonelier than men's.

XIII

Between the sedge and water's edge,
The clean white, the swan in flight.

Wan with long sorrows of men
I followed and found my mate again.

And then I knew I flew alone,
Alone, yet echoing of two.

Beyond the west, forget not thou,
O vanished swan, thy mate, that now
Must nest uneasy in my breast.

XIV

My love was blasted
By an oak
That sat on a silver hill
And never spoke,
Not a word said he
When we were lovers,
When the air was filled
With the rainy whistle
Of plovers.
Never a word said he
Though we desired
Our love with leafy music
Grandly choired.
Then the wind sang, the skies
Opened, and spoke;
Spoke in a lightning flash
And our love broke.
But never a leaf or a twig was injured then
On the singing oak.

XV

Paris was the comeliest man
That ever filched a wife,
But for each time he kissed his love
A Trojan lost his life.

Helen was the fairest lady
That ever bore the name,
But when she gave her to her love
All Troy burst into flame.

O I have died a Trojan's death
For every smallest joy.
Is it not time, my very love,
To fire the walls of Troy?

XVI

Here in the field beside the wood
The grass is withered where he stood
From dawn till dark day after day,
Watching and listening, until
Wasted with loneliness he lay
Under the autumn twilight-grey.
His sheep are scattered over the hill.

When eyes were blind and lips were dumb,
Then did she think of him, and come
Back to the pastureland they knew
And meet a phantom in the chill
Morass of sedges white with dew? —
But miles are long and years are few.
His sheep are scattered over the hill.

Here in the field beside the wood
The grass is withered where he stood.

XVII

Slender Naiad of stone
My kiss on your mouth
Smote me with cold.
Wake quickly! the dream we have known
Is a silver swan flying
Away to the south.
You have chilled all the air with your mouth,
And the garden is dying.

XVIII

Now on the idle pond
Slowly the fallen leaf
Drifts with its double.

Crescent from prow to poop,
Curving with curves of gold,
Galley of silence.

How have our pomps decayed!
Frail is the royal barge,
Autumn the cargo.

XIX

So soft in the hemlock wood
The phoenix sang his lullaby,
Shepherds drowsed where they stood,
Slumber felled each passerby,
And lovers at their first caress
Slept in virgin loneliness.

Not for mortal eye to see
Naked life arise from embers;
Only the dark hemlock tree,
Evergreen itself, remembers
How the Word came into being,
No man hearing, no man seeing.

From the taut bow of sleep
Shoots the phoenix toward the day,
Shepherds wake and call their sheep,
Wanderers go on their way.
Unaware how death went by,
Lovers under the hemlocks lie.

XX

Pan of the Crossroads, take the song
Thy pilgrim offers at the shrine.
It is the memory of one
Who at the rising of the sun
Went down the other road from mine.
It is a memory held too long;
Take thou the memory with the song.

XXI

The grapes are ripe, the frost is near,
The cricket sounds a rusty note,
And the bluebird at the close of year
Repeats the April song by rote.

Day still is warm, but after dark
Autumn advances leaf by leaf;
And the watchdog with a nervous bark
Halts an imaginary thief.

XXII

It is October in our hearts,
The vineyards of the years are ripe.
From thinning forests Pan departs,
And we shall never hear his pipe
Playing across the hill.

O it was well to drink our fill
Of pleasure while the sun was high,
And it is well beneath the still
Suspense of twilight-heavy sky
To drink our fill of sleep.

The hush that follows song is deep,
Far deeper than the song was gay,
And autumn pasturing ghostly sheep
Among the fields of yesterday
Is shepherd of our dreams.

Heap the dead leaves beside the streams
Where youth has heard the summer song;
Heap the bonfire that redeems
The dead who wake in light, and throng
The shadow where it darts. . . .
It is October in our hearts.

XXIII

Let us for ever be at peace
As walls and mountains are,
Or as the ocean storms that cease
When smoother tides would hold a star.
We strove with shadows for so long,
We sped our youth so fast,
But now the bell has rung for evensong
And sleep, at last.

How many frolics we have seen
Who now shall frisk no more,
And made pretense of budding green
When autumn ripened at the core.
When wit was wanting words were long
And folly made reply,
Now all our words are but good-night, our song
A lullaby.

XXIV

In solemn pause the forest waits
The signal to return;
Within our rotting garden gates
The weeds of autumn burn.

Father to son we held our field
Against the siege of tares,
Knowing our weaker sons would yield
The land no longer theirs.

Knowing how wind and sun and rain
Would fling their green stampedes
Where we who harvested the grain
Lie buried under weeds.

XXV

Shutters bang in the wind outside;
Cobwebs hang from the mildewed walls;
Stale, damp mould in the lifeless cold;
Doors flung wide to the darkened halls.

Love and strength of the new, keen race
Lie full length where the weeds grow high,
All things swept to the past except
This ruined place the wind roars by.

Blank disaster of empty windows;
Broken plaster strewn on the floor;
Darkness spills from the wild, bleak hills,
And the winter wind blows under the door.

XXVI

I have known the lure of cities and the bright gleam of
    golden things,
Spires, towers, bridges, rivers, and the crowd that flows as
    a river,
Lights in the midnight streets under the rain, and the
    stings
Of joys that make the spirit reel and shiver.

But I see bleak moors and marshes and sparse grasses,
And frozen stalks against the snow;
Dead forests, ragged pines, and dark morasses
Under the shadows of the mountains where no men go.
The crags untenanted and spacious cry aloud as clear
As the drear cry of a lost eagle over uncharted lands,
No thought that man has ever framed in words is spoken
    here;
And the language of the wind, no man understands.

Only the sifting wind through the grasses, and the hissing
    sleet,
And the shadow of the changeless rocks over the frozen
    wold,
Only the cold,
And the fierce night striding down with silent feet.

XXVII

Hunched at angles
Over new snow
The ironwood tree.
Crotch of bough
Tufted with snow
And nothing to see
Of leaf and of leaf
That a few weeks ago
Were the ironwood tree.
Skeleton now
It is bole and bough,
A perch for a crow
Or a chickadee
With feathers ruffed back
When the winds blow.
And below
There is only new snow
And nothing to see
Of leaf and of leaf
Or of you,
Or of me.

XXVIII

The snow lies crisp beneath the stars,
On roofs and on the ground,
Late footsteps crunch along the paths,
There is no other sound.

So cold it is the very trees
Snap in the rigid frost,
A dreadful night to think on them, —
The homeless and the lost.

The dead sleep sheltered in the tomb;
The rich drink in the hall;
The Virgin and the Holy Child
Crouch shivering in a stall.

XXIX

The winter night is hard as glass;
The frozen stars hang stilly down;
I sit inside while people pass
From the dead-hearted town.

The tavern hearth is deep and wide,
The flames caress my glowing skin;
The icicles hang cold outside,
But I sit warm within.

The faces pass in blurring white
Outside the frosted window, lifting
Eyes against my cheerful night,
From their night of dreadful drifting.

Sharp breaths blow fast in a smoky gale,
Rags wander through the dull lamp light;
O my veins run gold with Christmas ale,
And the tavern fire is bright.

The midnight sky is clear as glass,
The stars hang frozen on the town,
I watch the dying people pass,
And I wrap me warm in my gown.

XXX

The dark red winter woods are bleak
With something that they dare not speak.
Silent they stand, and will not stir
To greet the hurrying messenger
Who passes on across the hill,
Leaving them desolate and still.

What memories of summer hymns
Are frozen in those leafless limbs?
What secrets, folded in the bud,
Lie hidden, till the bursting flood
Of resurrection call them forth
When younger lovers wander north?

Yet, in this January hour,
We care not if tomorrow's flower
Waits eager-petaled to arise
Or with the dead for ever lies
Here in this quiet, lonely land,
Where dark red trees of winter stand.

A SONNET SEQUENCE

I

Quickly and pleasantly the seasons blow
Rippling the meadows of eternity,
As wave on wave the pulsings of the sea
Merge and are lost, each in the other's flow.
Time is no lover; it is only he
That is the one unconquerable foe,
He is the sudden tempest none can know,
Winged with swift winds that none may hope to flee.
But thou art my beloved; these endless fears
Are nought to us, let us be gods of stone,
And set our images above the years
On some high mount where we can be alone;
And thou shalt ever be as now thou art,
And I shall watch thee with untroubled heart.

II

Then judge me as you will, I can not flee;
I can not turn away from you for ever,
For there are bonds that wisdom can not sever,
And slaves with souls far freer than the free.
Such strong desires the Universal Giver
With unknown plan has buried deep in me,
That simply watching you has come to be
The sum and substance of my life's endeavour.
You weary of me, lingering so near,
I know the scorn you hide within your heart,
And yet, your face has never seemed so dear
As now, when I am minded to depart.
And though you drive me hence, I love you so
That I shall watch you when you do not know.

III

Strange to be loved by all the world but one,
And that one, loving once, now lost for ever;
Praise is a weary thing when praise is done,
And love from those unloved not worth endeavour.
Her waywardness one time toward me directed
Now leaves me to a semblance of acclaim;
Where no love is, no love can be expected,
However high once mounted her quick flame.
Burnt out and burning are conjoinëd ill;
And all the tinder offered to my fires
By others than this brand which flared so chill,
Is worse than substitute to my desires.
She, loving once, unloving now, is blasting
The hopes of those who fast for me, — the fasting.

IV

Even as love grows more I write the less,
Impelled to speak, when neither words nor voice
Possess a phrase to snare one of the joys
You, only you, so utterly possess.
Stay the bright swallow high in airy poise.
Carve statues of love's ultimate caress,
Gather the fruits of tears and happiness,
Make bloom for ever what one hour destroys,
Then shamed to speech by such unheard-of skill
I may find words to name you, and to sing
Such praises of your beauty as shall fill
The world with songs of all remembered spring.
Till then you are like starlight on the air,
Or clouds at dawn, unutterably fair.

V

Long after both of us are scattered dust
And later men perhaps shall read of thee
By time called to an alien century,
Time, love's ally, in whom love put no trust;
Who will these random hearts, these readers be?
Old men to laugh at us? or more unjust
Young men to read the syllables of lust
In what was love when it was surely we?
And yet a few there may be who will feel
Indwelling in these words their own desires
And reading them know that they but reveal
New images in the unchanging fires;
And they indeed will linger with a sigh
To think that beauty such as thine must die.

VI

Remembered spring redeems the withered year,
And wherefore should my spirit be afraid
Though autumn winds wail through the smoky shade
And chill me with this too prophetic fear.
I know that you and I and love must fade,
And what all youth is told, that must I hear,
How you whose loveliness I hold so dear,
Borrowed from dust, to ashes must be paid.
Yet linger still over these wasted meadows
Echoes of song and winter ghosts of flowers,
And from foreboding winds and early shadows
Come thoughts of other seasons, other hours.
Remembered spring the withered year redeems,
And we who sleep, sleep not without our dreams.

VII

This can not matter much; this dust and dust
Whirling together in the lap of spring;
This is one night, one hour, one moment, lust
Brought large to bloom, bursting, and withering.
This can not matter much; consider time
Feasting on history, and great cities spilled
Like crumbs about his table, the long climb
Of man from mud toward cities he can not build.
This can not matter much, this wandering hand
Moving across your body, nor the flung
Delights that overwhelm and die. The grand
Design moves onward with this thing unsung.
This can not matter; love conceals, death tells,
And yet there is nothing else, there is nothing else.

VIII

Today as I passed through the market-place,
I saw so many things that you might want;
Don't scold me, I was not extravagant, —
A few necessities, that's all, in case
You should be lonely: a papyrus plant
From Egypt; an old saint with a green face;
A unicorn, — quite tame; a bit of lace
Woven from cobwebs; and an elephant.
Please don't be cross; I sold a poem today,
And really you must have these useful things;
Look! here's the best of all; I can not say
Just what it is, but it has lovely wings,
Shines like a rainbow, too. Good God! it's gone.
Kiss me. Don't cry. I'll find another one.

IX

Yes, we have shared these things and loved them well,
Too well, perhaps, and they have come to seem
A part of us and merged into the scheme
Of life that flows beneath the frozen shell.
This room of ours, the lamplight's yellow gleam,
Our hands, the futile broken words that tell
Nothing and still show all, — these fragments dwell
In us, the very fabric of our dream.
And yet, — O do I fear or seek this truth? —
I know that when each turns aside his head
To scan the far horizon for his home,
These things will fall away from us as youth
Once fell away, and memory will be shed
Like blossoms when the time of fruit has come.

X

Only last night we dwelt together, we
Whose lips the kindliest farewells enthrall;
Last night itself is but a stone let fall
Into the chasm of eternity.
There shall be echoes, I shall hear them call
However faint, however far they be;
There shall be shadows, I shall always see
Them beckon from Time's memory-haunted hall.
The dear mirages of the years gone by
Glow falsely golden from their dark domain,
But now they move me not. " Mere mockery,"
Low to my heart I say to still its pain,
And cloud-built cities in the sunset sky
Fade out in dark across the endless plain.

XI

Peace be with you and blessing, and for me
The utter void of uneventful days
When all the passions are turned loose to graze
On stubble and the bark of fallen tree.
When love is gone the nervous spirit brays
Like a young calf weaned from maternity; —
O whet the knife! and we shall shortly see
A feast of veal to win a monarch's praise.
Then let us gluttonously feed on flesh
That once was ours for sensitive delight.
Come, add my wisdom and begin afresh
And make a meal on what began a bite.
Then with my passions and my wisdom slain,
I shall be ready when you come again.

XII

And now at sunset, ripples flecked with gold
Leap lightly over the profounder blue;
The wind is from the north, and days are few
That still divide us from the winter cold.
O, it was easy in the morning dew
To make the vow that never should be old,
But now at dusk the words are not so bold, —
Thus have I learned. How fares the hour with you?
A heron rises from the trembling sedge,
His vigil at an end. Mine too is done.
A late sail twinkles on the watery edge,
And up the shore lights sparkle one by one.
Seasons will change before tomorrow's sun,
So speaks the dune-grass on the windy ledge.

XIII

Last night I wrote a letter to my friend:
I said, " Come back, we two are getting old;
Our separate lives wear on; the years are cold,
And loneliness grows bitter toward the end."
I called you back, but you shall not behold
Those wise, sad words that my desire has penned;
Last night I wrote what I shall never send,
The page your white hands never shall unfold.
There in my desk it lies; pride guards the key;
And pride, alas, is stronger than desire.
Years hence perhaps some stranger, pityingly,
Will yield the faded secret to the fire,
Where it will join in dust those separate dead,
Sorrow who wrote and Love who never read.

XIV

Let those who love hear me; I speak as one
Who has known every portion of love's pain,
And all the swift delights that flare and wane
Between the setting and the rising sun.
Sins have I known whose sweetness left no stain,
And virtues that much villainy have done,
But now the pattern that my heart has spun
Is finished, and I see that it is vain.
Vain is the virgin kiss, and vain the thought
That binds the heart's desire from afar,
Each loves the image his own mind has wrought,
Each worships no true spirit, but a star.
By none is this believed, until the years
Reveal the sad deception, and with tears.

XV

O it was gay! the wilderness was floral,
The sea a bath of wine to the laughing swimmer;
Dawn was a flaming fan, dusk was a glimmer
Like undersea where sly dreams haunt the coral.
The garden sang of fame when the golden shimmer
Of sun glowed on the proud leaves of the laurel, —
But time and love fought out their ancient quarrel;
The songs are fainter now, the lights are dimmer.
For it is over, over, and the spring
Is not quite spring to you who sit alone;
A paradise entire has taken wing.
Love and her merry company are gone
The way of all delight and lyric measure,
And the lone miser mourns his vanished treasure.

XVI

At last, poor Love, I know your weary pain,
And what a noisome plague it is to be
Beloved by another; now I see
My past self in her folly mirrored plain.
She quotes and sombrely ascribes to me
Words that the maddest corner of this brain
Could never have brought forth, — or would;
    while she
Martyr to my ill faith, for faith is slain.
Before she dies, she yearns to see my face.
(Beware Sir Robert, death hath strange caprices.)
She keeps my letters in a holy place
(And hers I carefully tear in tiny pieces).
Dearest, was I like this in times gone by?
How kind you were! how imbecile was I!

XVII

The last debauch; tomorrow I shall go
Alone into the upper light, where dwells
Conjecture. There shall be no faint farewells
Or any leavetaking that mortals know.
Drink deep, drink deep, life's fathomable wells
Are almost dry. For at the first cock-crow
I shall stride forth and answer blow with blow
And dim the sun with brighter miracles.
Nothing will go with me but wrath I glean
Among these meadows where we plant no joys;
May pride be in my hands a sword as keen
As is the flash that blesses and destroys.
And so, Farewell! the highway that I tread
Is dark or dawn, the living! — or the dead!

XVIII

It is not, Death, that we resent your power;
Life moves by that as well as by increase,
But you invade our welfare and our peace,
You threaten us before your appointed hour.
We know you, sombre master of release
From all the sick repinings that devour
Our later years, but why should you deflower
Our youth as well, and bid the music cease?
God knows the ages of our kind are dust;
We drift from war to war, from hate to hate,
And all our loves still falter into lust;
But there are rifts among the clouds of fate
Through which the sun might come if you would wait,
And let us dance our moth-dance down the gust.

XIX

Men lied to them and so they went to die.
Some fell, unknowing that they were deceived,
And some escaped, and bitterly bereaved,
Beheld the truth they loved shrink to a lie.
And those there were that never had believed,
But from afar had read the gathering sky,
And darkly wrapt in that dread prophecy,
Died hoping that their truth might be retrieved.
It matters not. For life deals thus with Man;
To die alone deceived or with the mass,
Or disillusioned to complete his span.
Thermopylae or Golgotha, all one,
The young dead legions in the narrow pass;
The stark black cross against the setting sun.

XX

The spring blew low, the spring demanded mirth,
With childish song and fingers in my hair.
I turned to stone, and dully wondered where
You would find comfort over all the earth.
Friend of my love, mute brother of my sadness,
The meddling season can but touch anew
My broken strings to discord, but for you
There is escape from all this sultry madness.
" I went but I return." A gust of rain
Blew down the sky and faltered into mist.
" Let me come back and weep with you again."
Spring had no folly like a lovers' tryst.
I saw in the young lips she may have kissed
Another's tragic mouth at peace with pain.

XXI

Through the deep night the leaves speak, tree to tree;
Where are the stars? the frantic clouds ride high,
The swelling gusts of wind blow down the sky
Shaking the thoughts from the leaves, garrulously.
Through the deep night, articulate to me,
They question your untimely passing by;
Your spring was still in flower, must you fly
Windswept so soon down lanes of memory?
Through the deep night the trees recount the past,
The lovers that have long ago gone hence
And whom you joined ere love had reached its prime.
Chill with an early autumn's immanence,
Through the dark night plunges the sudden blast,
Sweeping the young leaves down before their time.

XXII

So ends the day with beauty in the west,
Bending in holy peace above the land;
It is not needful that we understand;
Oblivion is ours, and that is best.
Oblivion of battles that command
Our wan reluctance, and a starless rest
Borne on in tideless twilight, where all quest
Ends in the pressure of a quiet hand.
There is no morrow to this final dream
That paints the past so wonderfully fair;
No rising sun shall desecrate that gleam
Of fragile colour hanging in the air.
Enshrined in sunset are all things that seem
Happy and beautiful, — and Thou art there.

XXIII

Calmer than mirrored waters after rain,
Calmer than all the swaying tides of sleep,
Profounder than the stony eyes that keep
Afternoon vigil on the ruined plain;
So drift they by, the cloudy forms that creep
In stealthy whiteness through the windless grain;
The twilight ebbs, and washed in the long rain,
I am their shepherd, pasturing my sheep.
They can not change; they can but wander here;
That is their destiny and also mine;
The fuel that I was, the flames they were,
Are vanished down the lost horizon line.
Likewise the stars have died; the silence hears
Only the footfall of the pastured years.

XXIV

The mirrors of all ages are the eyes
Of some remembering god, wherein are sealed
The beauties of the world, the April field,
Young faces, blowing hair, and autumn skies.
The mirrors of the world shall break, and yield
To life again what never really dies;
The forms and colours of earth's pageantries
Unwithered and undimmed shall be revealed.
And in that moment silence shall unfold
Forgotten songs that she has held interred,
The ocean rising on the shores of gold,
Flecked with white laughter and love's lyric word;
All happy music that the world has heard;
All beauty that eternal eyes behold.

XXV

Love dwelled with me with music on her lips;
Beauty has quickened me to passion; prayer
Has cried from me before I was aware,
When grief was scourging me with scarlet whips.
The gods gave me to follies false and fair,
Made me the object of immortal quips,
But I am recompensed with comradeships
The gods themselves would be content to share.
The time of play has been, of wisdom, is;
Yet who can say which is the truly wise?
Enough that I have stayed love with a kiss,
That kindness has found welcome in my eyes;
Though the long poplar path leads dark before,
Up to the white inevitable door.

XXVI

There is a void that reason can not face,
Nor wisdom comprehend, nor sweating will
Diminish, nor the rain of April fill, —
And I am weary of this wan grimace.
Behold I touch the garments of all ill
And do not wash my hands; a dusty place
Unprobed by light becomes a loud millrace
That swirls together straw and daffodil.
It is untrue that vigil can not trace
The orbits which upon our births distill
The filtered dew of fate; I saw the hill
That I must climb, and gauged the upward pace;
And now upon the night's worn windowsill
I wait and smile. Hail, Judas, full of grace.

XXVII

Some of that August day's long dead delight
Came back to me, as on a winter hill
I saw red sunset fall away, and spill
Its scattered jewels on the lap of night.
We two had always been so calm, so still,
That silence was not lonely, and in spite
Of shadow deepening over snowy white,
A warmth, as of your presence, smote the chill.
Whatever men may call the real, the true,
This much I know indeed, that an immense
And actual radiance such as only you
Have ever given to my mortal sense
Gleamed on the hillside and then vanished hence;
And all that winter night the south wind blew.

XXVIII

" Now all the autumn night is vast and still,
Curled round our feet in valleys white with haze,
And from the tall composure of this hill
We watch the constellations go their ways.
Below the dead are sleeping in their shrouds,
Nor ever wake to shadow our delight;
And quiet as the dead, the alien crowds
Slumber in ashen cities all the night.
We two alone are living, we alone
Sail on the world's high deck through starry seas.
Nourished by love, our human souls have grown
Into the stature of divinities.
We two are Life; all else is past and dead. . . ."
Who spake these words? what mean the things he said?

MISCELLANEOUS SONNETS

Portrait

Quick with your paints and palette there! the colour
Ebbs from my languid arteries. Be quick!
I feel my hair grow grey, my eyes grow duller,
And all the youthful contour blurred and thick.
I hear your nervous brushes rub and click,
Racing with time to catch my brief reflection,
And keenly hear the numbered minutes tick,
Outdistancing your patience for perfection.
Can you retrace the mask of life, the section
Of universal chaos that is I?
The scars of flame, the gleams of resurrection
From loves that wither into lusts that die?
O do be quick! before these vanish hence,
Leaving a blank of bland indifference.

Casino

In Monte Carlos of the sky I tossed
My savings down, even my hopes of winning;
Worlds flickered, and I knew that I had lost
Before the vast roulette had ceased from spinning.
I can't accuse the Croupier of fraud,
Though Time, his bouncer, is a hooligan,
And Luck, his serving woman, is a bawd; —
These are immortal; I am but a man.
Of course, I could go bankrupt and produce
Sole asset, just one little piece of lead,
But I suspect that all too simple ruse
Would treble my indebtedness. Instead
I'll pay him day by day the total score,
Bet life again, — and lose it as before.

From the Foothills

By many paths we reach the single goal,
And all our quarrels deal but with its name;
There is no soul so different from my soul
As in its essence to be not the same.
No warrior but in his heart must know
How triumph is not proud nor vengeance sweet,
For he beholds, who slays the kindred foe,
Himself, self-murdered, lying at his feet.
It has been written that we are the islands
Which, ocean-sundered into seeming twain,
Are truly of one continent, the highlands
Wrought of one rock and rooted in one plain.
Bright Himalayan peace! the humblest crest
One with the splendour of Mount Everest.

Platitude

Dull platitude, worn coin from wisdom's mint,
You purchase still your phrase's worth of truth
While clever counterfeits for all their glint
Buy but the penny sophistries of youth.
Lacklustre, thin, the date illegible,
Scarred by the teeth of every sceptic age,
Your metal still rings true as when it fell
New-moulded from the furnace of a sage.
The novelty of noon is out of date
By night; the timeless gold, however worn,
In undiminished worth will circulate
From hands long dust to others yet unborn.
Let counterfeiters buy the world! The wise
Save thriftily for larger merchandise.

Overheard

The grey sea beach was empty but for three
Who paced the foamline of the rising tide.
The two, mother and son, looked out to sea,
The third, invisible, walked at their side.
He shouted to them. (Hear the salt wind sighing.)
He wrung his hands. (The air is growing chill.)
He cried aloud, " You see the grey gull flying,
Can't you see me, Matilda? Can't you, Bill? "
A sudden notion swept into her head:
" You look more like your father all the time."
" I don't! I look just like myself," he said,
And then both smiled like partners in a crime.
The third was writhen into wisps of pain
And scattered into the grey fog again.

With Simple Words

With simple words to say a simple thing
He would have charmed away your year of woe,
But when he spoke it was a violin string
Which snapped to the full urging of the bow.
Or was it you who shut your ears, and so
Denied old beauties that are contraband;
To whom the old spirit sang in vain, although
You pry the flesh of dead kings from the sand?
With silent lips now and with empty hand
He walks among you vulnerable to scorn,
Yet thinking of the twilight in that land
And listening for his comrade's evening horn,
And wondering of that day when he was born
To write these words you will not understand.

More

Always more riches, more enjoyment, more
Of everything the world can briefly give,
Though through your avid hands as through a sieve
Beauties unnumbered and unnoticed pour.
You chase the wind, but you are fugitive
From the great quiet at the whirlwind's core,
And spendthrift of life's measurable store
You have not purchased the mere right to live.
There is a vacant seat beside me here
Where you may rest and watch the season change;
Form, colour, tone, mysterious or clear,
In swift variety though never strange,
Where if one beauty wholly be revealed
Life will have yielded all she has to yield.

Fire Music

From the blue air where you have wandered free
I call you home to slumber and forget;
Down the white drift of stars I cast my net
And draw you inward from the breathing sea.
The mist is rising where the sun has set,
The laden cobweb sags from tree to tree;
All have gone home now, Child, but you and me; ——
Wherefore this terror and this wan regret?
I could not give you life, I could but lend;
Yet lest the night be long I kindle now
Flame after flame around you to defend
Your quiet heart and your untroubled brow,
And I have sealed your silence with a vow:
Love shall return to wake you in the end.

Take Thou These Flowers

Take thou these flowers from gardens where the streams
Have suffered drought, where spring has been unkind;
Take thou these songs from one who can not bind
Smooth harmonies to his disordered themes.
Take thou these poems, although the craftsman seems
Incapable of what his soul designed;
And, though the nightmare oft possess his mind,
Take thou the nightmare with his happier dreams.
More than this love I offer thou hast much:
Pleasure and praise, worship of nobler men;
Yet I aspire, though character and pen
Miss thee by leagues of altitude, to touch
Thy life, and having touched it, to possess,
Leaving thee poor amidst my lavishness.

He Who in Spring's Rebirth

He who in spring's rebirth has put his trust
Now answers not to April or to May,
Nor sees the moon-white apple blossom sway,
Nor breathes its sweetness on the evening gust.
He who was first to climb the height of day
Lies full-length in the valley of the dust;
His sword sleeps in his hand, and it is rust;
His heart sleeps in his breast, and it is clay.
Brother, so mute among the fallen years,
We come at dayspring to your living tomb
That is the green earth, and we shed no tears,
Knowing that if you wander otherwhere
Soon will you give us gracious welcome there,
And if you perished, then we share your doom.

Repartee

As one bears beneath his neighbour's roof
Some thrust that staggers his unready wit,
And brooding through the night on such reproof
Too late conceives the apt reply to it;
So all our life is but an afterthought,
A puzzle solved long past the time of need,
And tardy wisdom that one failure bought
Finds no occasion to be used in deed.
Fate harries us; we answer not a word,
Or answering too late, we waste our breath;
Not even a belated quip is heard
From those who bore the final taunt of death;
And thus the Jester parries all retort:
His jest eternal, and our lives so short.

This Leaf Has Fallen

This leaf has fallen, and that leaf, this leaf and that,
This leaf has fallen, that leaf has fallen, and this,
It can't be long now, but trees do not miss
Leaves any more than skeletons their fat.
They leaf again. The resurrection is
At springtime for them all. Their windy chat
Will make next summer clamorous. But what
Spring shall renew us? Men are not like trees.
This leaf has fallen, and that. But no buds lurk
Beneath our leaves. We shall not leaf again.
Within us winter and the north wind work
Their gradual havoc on the lives of men.
Somehow it does not matter. Somehow it is
Restful to think that men are not like trees.

LONGER POEMS

The Halt in the Garden

Hesperides? Right here! the faithful keeper,
Sir, at your service. Won't you step this way?
The shadows round the elm are growing deeper,
You can not go much farther on today.
Sit here, this rock will hold the heat a while,
And later, if you're so inclined, we'll sup
Over at my house in the hollow there.
It must be you I saw that clambered up
The rock-ledge and came through the broken stile?
The other road is shorter by a mile,
But you are young, — I don't suppose you care.

Yes, help yourself, but don't take three or four;
Take one and eat it to the very core.
Hell! that young Pan's a scoundrel! Nibbles one,
Throws it away, nibbles another, shakes
The bough, — and nine times out of ten it breaks, —
Spilling my finest beauties by the score
To rot away and stink under the sun.
These be no common apples; — no, not gold,
If people said so then it's lies they told, —
They're all the seasons bottled in one fruit,
Autumn atop and April at the root.
And what a savour to the nose and tongue!

No, Sir, I never touch them, I am here
To guard not eat . . . but once, O years ago,
Long before you were thought of . . . well, I know
Their taste and smell, and I should still be young
If I had gone on eating year to year.

The gods, now, 'tis their right, but even they
Come seldom. Not that I'm complaining, only
As I grow old I seem to grow more lonely.
Life isn't as it was for them or me;
There's more time to remember, less to play,
And somehow one pretends at being gay.
When they have picnics by the linden tree
Across the valley, one or two come over
And lie here at my feet among the clover,
Picking the petals off the daisies, while
I tell them fairy tales to make them smile.
For, between us, Sir, they are children still,
Ready to burst with laughter as with tears,
In spite of all that time has done, — and will.

I've loved them now over three thousand years,
And served them as you see, not well or ill,
And I can tell you, Sir, my blood runs cold
To think I shall be dead when they are old.
O most of all, Hermes and Artemis
I love, — the immortal Girl, the immortal Boy!

To see them is a sort of awful joy,
To touch them, unimaginable bliss.
Many have tried to snare them, and in vain;
For when you spread the usual sort of mesh,
Music and wine to catch them, then they are
As ghostly and remote as the white train
Of seven moons that swarm about the star
Of Zeus. White flame of spirit and of mind,
Held in twin columns of triumphant flesh!
And yet, they say how each has given his heart
Unto the other, and how they take their joys
Touching with one aerial kiss, to part
She with her virgins, he among his boys. . . .
You smile that love so far outdoes my wit,
Words being finite and love infinite.

Compare with these immortals, if you will,
The latter pieties I entertain.
They mope along the summit of the hill
As though the landscape pleased them not, and strain
To find a blemish on my apple trees, —
A blemish! here in the Hesperides!
I vow, Sir, it's my duty I perform,
And neither more nor less, when that pale swarm
Come buzzing down on me and call me Brother
As though it were a virtue so to do!
We take our liberties in all the ranks,

But none takes liberties with any other, —
You understand, Sir, — well, this pious crew,
Instead of dining in the hall outside,
Invite themselves to take their meat with me,
Seeming to think I ought to render thanks
Because they sacrifice my servant's pride
To make a show of their humility!
By Hera! then my blood all turns to gall, . . .
I serve cold porridge in the outer hall.

No tolerant stream can ever irrigate
Those arid minds. No kindly flower or shrub
Wakes on those desert hearts. Early and late
The scorpion and the unwholesome grub
Gnaw round the cactus and the prickly thorns.
Why, Sir, that aged Jew who wears the horns, —
His name escapes me, — played so vile a trick
That even Ares wept to hear the tale.
He found young Arothyx, Campaspe's faun,
Playing all naked in the woods at dawn
Beside the tarn, the way our children do.
What then? the old man took a briary stick
And laid it on his haunches like a flail
Until the creature was all black and blue,
His infant flesh shot through and through with hurt.
It's blame and scold from dawn to dark, and still
Despising, they remain to vent despite.

We plant the rose and they unearth the dirt.
There is no peace upon the sacred hill,
No songs at noon or drinking bouts at night.
It's not " Do as you please and so will I,"
But " Do my will; if not, be damned thereby."
Some of my Greeks are lechers and all that,
But every one's a born aristocrat!

The curious thing is this: that gentle man
They call their Master, is a different kind.
He comes to supper with me when he can,
And eats there in my room, but I don't mind.
He doesn't pose and condescend to me,
But just as any friend to friend might be,
Sits down and eats, asks me about the weather,
Are apples ripe? and how is Aphrodite
Since her last lying-in? No high and mighty
From him; he's just a dreamy sort of friend,
Not hard to talk with or to comprehend.
The only time he ever lost his head
Was once when we were talking here together,
I told about his people. Then he said . . .
Perhaps I ought not tell you what he said,
But if words kill those holy goats are dead!

Forgive me, Sir, an old man, the late year,
We all drift on, and night is close at hand.

141

The planets now are ripe, harvest is near,
And they will sow new planets where we stand.
See there, the flock of yellow butterflies
That chase September down the western slope
Have flashed their last against the smoky skies.
Your hand, Sir, if you please. Blear eyes must grope
And clear still lead. . . . Hark! do you hear them
    shouting
Over the hill where the red sun has set?
While we sit here conjecturing and doubting
The gods of Greece are gods of laughter yet.
Over the hill, the young with blowing hair
Forget the season of the singing reapers
Who come to bind the yellow planets in.
Forget the season of the silent sleepers,
The ruined barn, the harvest in the bin.

Come in, and drink and eat, and still forgive
That lonely age should be so talkative.
I'll quench the burning itch that jerks my tongue
In draughts of wine that still remembers Greece,
And you shall hear but silence while you sup.
Once in this garden when the world was young,
At cool of evening . . . No, I'll hold my peace!
Yonder's a Chian vintage. Fill your cup!

Prothalamion

Lamp of the West, held high aloft
By hand unseen of her whose name
Thou bearest; star when nights are soft
And earth breathes skyward the faint flame
Of pungent green wherein is mingled
Wild cherry's virginal, keen smell;
White Venus, singled
From galaxies to be the guide
Of man and bride,
Take thou our thanks for this thy miracle.

The silver-footed girl once crept
And leaned far out the window ledge
To ponder when they thought she slept,
Thy twin lights at the water's edge;
Until as sparks among the embers
Die, thine image waned away,
But she remembers,
And for the wonder thou hast wrought
A votive thought
She offered on the threshold of the Day.

Yet spring was late this year; the snow
Still hid thee and the garden paled

Beneath a withered moon, as though
For once thy miracle had failed.
Thin oak leaves, ghosts of foliage, clung
Above the new year in the sheath,
And where they hung
Cold shadow hid the snow from day
So that it lay
Round every tree-trunk like a faded wreath.

Now comes thine hour. This marriage eve
Will I alone thy vigil keep,
While maiden-fingered fancies weave
For her upon the loom of sleep
Pictures of the inviolate land
More beautiful than snow, where she
Needs not my hand
To guide her, where she reigns in light
One last, long night,
Untrammeled by our fair conspiracy.

While I, leaning against the wicket,
Watch thy reflection in the pond,
And feel a rhythm through grass and thicket —
My pulse of life, swelling beyond
My veins, beating through space and far
Away where even thy glories blur,
O chosen star!

Yet she eludes us still this hour;
A chaster power
Than ours fills all the universe with her.

But thou and I shall call her back.
Love swoons in those vast periods;
Her feet stray in the heaving black
So far from the more homely gods.
O call her as she comes to me
Tomorrow in the lovers' dawn,
Clean as the sea,
Her gainly body tense with a surmise
That veils her eyes,
Not furtive but most regally withdrawn.

Behind her morning overarches,
Tiers of crimson fire that make
Greener the violent green of larches,
Bluer the calm blue of the lake.
The white swan drifts in mirrored sleep,
The haze is tangled in the rushes;
Clear and deep
A drop of dew rings in the pond
And fields respond
With songs of robins, meadowlarks, and thrushes.

Now, Love, I call thee, and am heard
By none but thee, I speak thy name;

I wed thee with a secret word
In accent quiet as a flame.
I say thou art the one who arrives
For ever, who never shall depart;
Through a thousand lives
When fields are sweetened beneath the sun
Thou art the one
Who wakes the immortal in the mortal heart.

Hasten! the world will crowd us in
With trumpet blast and wedding guest;
The loud solemnities begin,
The caravans come from the west;
The ships of sandalwood that smell
Sweet as the frankincense they bear
Drift on the swell
Like phantoms through the early haze,
Their lamps ablaze,
Their red sails flat against the moveless air.

Hasten! we have not long against
That hour of pomp when we must see
Our rocky garden neatly fenced,
Our love in mild captivity.
Now dawn spreads open like a fan
Of sultry fire, the wet leaves stir;
Girl and man

Pass through the elemental gate,
For spring was late
And now the summer has caught up with her.

At the waterside a tree is growing
Whose blossoms crowd the drifting air,
And of its fruit there is no knowing
Till thou hast tasted of it there.
Its dark leaves in the morning chime
Not of the morning or the night,
But of the time
Between the chaos and the flame
When softly came
The Word that made eternal love's delight.

Eternal the brief joy of flesh,
The finite infinite and whole,
The thwarted body fired afresh
By flames that mount into the soul.
The fruit shall follow the tree-in-flower
With ripe fulfilment after pain;
This is the hour,
The golden rift in time wherefrom
Surely shall come
The song of love-in-death made life again.

But thou, so young; more meet for thee
The birches tossing their green hair!

What blossom crowns the darker tree —
Joy? But thy pain I can not share.
This night I yield thee back to sleep,
This night, the last of loneliness,
I fold thee deep
In peace and ask no more until
Dawn floods the hill,
Not even thy phantom-self for a caress.

And now the curved horizon covers
Love's star that melts away in light.
Lamp of the West, fail not thy lovers
When after another day, the night
Shall lift thee in its arms, and I
In mine shall hold thy counterpart,
Thou in thy sky
And we in ours, until we rest
Beyond the west
Where death lies slain beneath the single heart.

Prothalamion

II

The hills turn hugely in their sleep
With sound of grinding rock and soil
While down their granite shoulders leap
The waterbrooks in white turmoil.
The vigil of Good Friday done,
Our second spring ascends the height;
The earth turns southward toward the sun,
And trees which guard the pascal door,
In leaf once more,
Once more are murmurous with strange delight.

For now is the world's Eastertide,
And born that they may die again
Arise from death the gods who died.
Osiris, slender as young grain,
Comes back to Isis; the shy lad
Adonis wakens by the stream;
And Jesus, innocently clad
In samite, walks beneath the trees,
Half ill-at-ease
That Judas and the Cross were but a dream.

And thou art she whom I have seen
Always, but never understood,

In broken shrines festooned with green,
In twilight chapels of the wood;
Or on the hills a shepherdess
Walked with the sun full on her face,
And though her body and her dress
Apparelled her in meek disguise,
I dropped my eyes,
For still I knew the goddess by her pace.

I know thee now in morning light
Though thou are wrought of flesh and blood,
And though the mother of the night
Resumes at dawn her maidenhood;
And though love severed with his knife
The girdle of the million years
And yielded to importunate life
The toll she asks of those who still
Would journey, till
They pass her known and visible frontiers.

The children from beyond the sun
Come bounding down the hillside grass,
And in the joyous rout is one
Who smiles and will not let us pass.
He stands, the fairest of them all,
And in his loveliness I trace
Thy loveliness. His light footfall

Bends not the grass he treads upon;
But he is gone
Before my eyes have feasted on his face.

Let him go back beyond the air;
This spring is ours, it is not his;
Those eager lips would take their share
Of love's yet undiminished kiss.
Fairer than he, as young, as gay,
As much a child, forget all things,
All but this transitory day
Of love, all things but love, and give
Thy fugitive
Delights to me who fly but with thy wings.

In undulant desire we merge,
On tides of light we sport and rest;
We swerve up from the deeper surge
To hover on the trembling crest
Of joy, and when the wave has passed,
Then smooth is the swing to the abyss
Of quietness, where with a last
Eye-darkening smile, we say farewell
Until the spell
Shall be renewed. Forget all things but this.

No grass-blade bends, no shadow stirs;
Love mounted high, slumber is deep;

Deep is the spring beneath the firs,
A sweet and lonely place for sleep.
And waking, we shall cool our flesh
In depths so clear they seem as air;
Twofold in beauty, thou refresh
Thy body in that water, bright
With muted light,
And brighter still for thy reflection there.

While I along the bank shall find
The flowers that opened with the day
Still dew-drenched, and with these entwined
New fronds of fern or darker bay.
Or pausing in a shaft of sun
That strikes across the mottled glade
Watch thee too long, beloved one,
Watch thee with eyes grown big with tears
Because the years
Suddenly spoke and made my heart afraid.

Giver of immortality —
That was thy name within the shrine —
The Mighty Mother, Star of the Sea,
All syllables of love were thine
To wear as lesser women wear
The garlands of their fragile spring;
Why then within my heart this fear

Of time? why then amid the shout
Of life, this doubt
That clouds the new sun like an outspread wing?

We must not to a foe like time
Yield up our present. Take my hand
And up the morning we shall climb
Until the wooded valley land
Lies all beneath us in the drowse
Of love's meridial aftermath;
The trellis of entwining boughs
Trembles in the great joy of green,
But does not screen
The comfortable glimpse of homeward path.

We will not to our ancient foe
Yield up this happiness; it lies
Shielded from sickle and from snow
And all the menace of the skies.
At night I shall watch over thee,
The future safe beneath thy breast,
And after autumn there shall be
Dayspring, when for each other's sake
We shall awake
And follow Love beyond the unknown west.

Ballad

As I was faring through a wood
Bewildered as I was,
I came upon a wayside rood
That glistered clear as glass.

Like glass in noontide sun, the rays
Stood out in thorny light
So dazzling to my darkened gaze
I could not see aright.

Why is the wonder wrought for me
So lost and so alone?
I knelt beneath the fiery tree
Upon a floor of stone.

Why for a man of little faith
This wonder for a saint?
A roof shut out the sky; beneath
The gloaming wood grew faint.

Low voices murmured and I heard
Bells far away and soft,
The lights around the rood were stirred
By smoke that swirled aloft.

The Host and the angelic Cup
Shone forth with forkëd flame,
But no priest came to lift them up
Or call them by their Name.

And there were others in that place
Who knelt or moved about,
And I beheld on every face
The secret smile of doubt.

And three with leaden measures crept
To prove the things of gold,
And one in robes of purple slept
Twitching as if with cold.

And as I watched, I saw a rout
Of beasts that trampled down
The three with rules who crept about,
The one who had a crown.

Oxen there were, and kine, and sheep,
That trampled down the men;
I shall not see unless in sleep
The like of that again.

But at the altar, pair by pair,
They bent, and so a yoke
Was placed upon them, made of air
Yet heavier than oak.

And all their bleating din grew still.
They stood in meek array
As if they waited there until
The break of Judgment Day.

Sanctus! the voice was like a star
Singing in silver curve.
A bell rang soft and very far
Yet rang through every nerve.

Sanctus! now farther and forlorn,
As if none understood.
The Host by hand unseen was borne
In glory to the rood.

Three times the bell rang out; it seemed
Each tinkle of the sound
Turned to a silent light that gleamed
Upon a holy ground.

The sanctus died upon my ear
And wakened on my eye
To be a star set high and clear
Amid a frightened sky.

The walls, the rood, the altar waned,
The chapel was no more;
Only the patient beasts remained
Where they had been before.

And where the altar once had stood
Came forth a maid who smiled;
And from the waning of the rood
Was born a laughing child.

" Mother," he said, " the day has come! "
Her face grew dark with pain.
" Mother, do thou and I go home,"
And she was healed again.

Then spread the angel of the east
Her wings of fire and gold.
Then vanished maid and child and beast,
And all the wood grew cold.

As cold as on a ruined hearth
The ashes of content;
As cold as the lost heart of earth
Whose inner warmth is spent.

As cold as he who saw the sight
And went upon his way
Denying, in the depth of night,
That he had seen the day.

Manorbier

(*To Mr. and Mrs. Arthur Machen*)

It is green with ivy
But the stones are criss-crossed
With cracks and crannies,
Tooth-marks of the frost;
The roofless tower,
The sundered wall,
The gaping lancet,
Frost gnaws them all.
Time in transit
Measured by years
Has emptied the hall,
Rusted the spears.
The long rains fall
Where the marriage bed
Saw the virgin a wife
And the mother dead,
Saw the birth of the son
And the warrior head
White on the pillow
Stained with red.

Now it is summer
The swans float

Each with its double
On the scummy moat.
If you hear the fiddler
Playing his fiddle
It's the wind in the crannies
With dust in its throat.
If you hear the drummer
Tapping his drum
It's a dead branch hanging
Swinging and banging,
Summoning no one,
There is no one to come.

I was born in a chamber
Under the eaves;
The room I remember
And the sound of leaves
And the sound of ocean
And ships come home
When we ran with our welcome
Knee-deep through foam.

With toy sword brandished
And toy horn blowing,
Child cries to the father,
" The old raven is dead! "
And the father to the child:

" Your mother is dead! "
And somebody said,
" He speaks of the raven
When his mother is dead."

In the garden by moonlight
Each leaf on the rose-bush
A silver flake,
A ghost of a flame!
Hearing voices, the loveless one
Fired by their passion
Fled down to the lake
Where a tall lady came.

"Tomorrow at sunset,"
She said to her lover,
" Look up to my window
And I will be there."
She glimmered away,
And faint like a halo
The moon on her hair.
Most beautiful lady,
How slowly the snail
Through the grey dust lengthens
His rainbow trail.
On the steps of the sunset
Did I find you — or not?

How should you remember
When your lover forgot?

Is there nobody now
Who can speak with my speech
But the wind in the ruin,
The waves on the beach?
There are hundreds of cities
Out there beyond reach,
Three thousand miles over
The sea whence I came.
I built them myself,
I left this to the weather
And forgot my own name.

I will go up the stairway
That ends in the air,
I will stand in the chapel
And offer a prayer
To saints who for ages
Have not been there.
I will lean out of windows
That have no top
And look far below me
A dizzy drop
To the moat and the cliff
And beyond to the beach

And beyond to the ocean
Where the eyes stop.

Why did I leave
   this house like a Viking?
Why did I leave it
   for frosts to crack?
Did the stairway lead me
   then to disaster?
Did the door ajar
   show the flame and the rack?
I have forgotten the cause of my going,
And even the cause of my coming back.

Some things with me
   are the never-dying,
All of us cursëd
   with time's effacement;
The ivy-vine grown
   so black has forgotten
The beginning tendril
   that clung to the basement;
The gap in the wall has forgotten the window,
And I, the face that looked down from the casement.

Now is the season when the whole world over
The herds are munching the ripe clover;

The green baby-hair of the crops to come
Is ruffled by the wind; the may-flies hum
In the air, and the bees intermittently humming
Dive to one flower and drone to a sweeter;
This is the mating-song season, at evening
When the lover listens his love will be coming.

But summer like winter
Conspiring slowly
To throw down the mighty
And exalt the lowly
Is gnawing at walls
All but time held holy.
By tendrils of ivy
The stones are split;
Trees shoulder the ingles
Where earls would sit,
And the ants drag the mortar
Away, bit by bit.

Who is my brother?
Who is my friend?
The song does not falter
Though the singer end.
But I, the last singer,
Forgetting my song
One summer morning

A thousand years long,
Have gone up the stairway
That ends in the air,
Surprising dead saints
With the ghost of a prayer,
And looked out of windows
That have no top,
To the beach, to the ocean,
Where the eyes stop.
But the mind will not stop.
The heart will not stop.

THE GATES OF THE COMPASS

I

Memory

The huntsman riding through the fogs of dawn
Lifts to his lips the horn of twisted gold
And blows two bell-like notes through glen and hollow
Mournfully keen as smoke of autumn leaves.
For ever young he rides a dying horse,
For ever on the chase though no stag flies,
Attended only by those double echoes
The soul and flesh, the day and night of time.
Until the blindfold of the fog between
His eyes and the far reaches of the day
Grows thin, and all around him he beholds
A countryside bathed in the light of dream.
And there dismounting, he goes forth alone
And blows the single golden note of peace.

If from all memories you ravelled one
Down the dark labyrinth of mind, what doors
Would open and what vistas be revealed
Among the many pasts you have forgotten?
I ask you of your birthplace, and you tell
Of leafy streets, a frame house on a terrace,
An apple tree with boughs that touched the ground
And made a cave of cider-smelling earth.

But dive beneath your thoughts. There you remember
The new-flung planet flaming into space
When it gave birth to something kin to you
In the dim dawn of life. Dive farther yet
And you will find perhaps like a deep pearl
Sunk under leagues of troubled sea, your self.
If from all memories you ravelled one
You could return behind time's double rhythm
And casting off the blindfold walls of space
Look clearly on what now is mystery.
But memory is frail and tenuous,
An evening cobweb drifting on the air
That weaves a rainbow down its wavering length,
Divides, entangles other strands, till soon
You are enmeshed in clinging gossamers
So subtle that to bind one to a thought
Were to destroy the airy fantasy.

Two bells that ring through fog, — what sorrow moves
Uneasily behind the curtained years?
Follow that memory until you see
A small boy grimy with the July heat
Sitting disconsolate upon the steps,
His eyes full, his chin cupped in his hands;
O many years ago, and yet you find
Your heart not uncompassionate of his.
The air was milky with the powder smoke

From firecrackers. All the afternoon
Two slow bells, tuned a minor third apart,
Clang after clang rang out the solemn news:
The Spanish fleet is sunk, the Spanish fleet
Is sunk at Santiago. . . . The Spanish fleet,
The Spanish fleet is sunk at Santiago.
The tears stung through the grime upon your cheeks
And you were dully sure that through all time
This sorrow would not fade. Those were your ships
That had been sunk, you loved their sounding names
And all their strangeness; they were proud and golden
Armadas on the oceans of your fancy,
Freighted with the imaginings of days,
Each day a lifetime; now they were yours no longer,
Nor ships, nor cargo, nor the dreams of them.
The elegant *Vizcaya,* curved and gilded,
The slim *Teresa,* her long masts aslant,
The *Almirante Oquendo,* high of prow,
The *Cristobal Colon,* her funnels set
Rakishly fore and aft the single mast,
And the destroyers, *Pluton* and *Furor,*
The pitiful, the vincible armada,
Scarce worth the Sunday morning's target practice.
You knew them all from keel to fighting-tops,
And saw the dawn-red waters of the harbour
As one by one against the shoreline hills
The doomed ships poured to gain the open sea.

The flames leapt from their funnels as they flew
And the foam fountained in a double jet
Before their prows; but speed, desperate speed
Was quite in vain. The grey ships hemmed them in.
The first gun boomed, a hundred others answered,
And the air whined and flickered with the shells.
As the first courser in a cavalry charge
Struck by a bullet jumps into the air
And stumbles to his death, the stricken ships
Reared to the sheet of flame, wallowed, and swung
In aimless curves, then brandishing their masts
Against the sky, cast up their gilded sterns
And burst with dull explosions undersea.
The two bells of that shabby triumph clang,
Still clang, the bells of victory still clang,
Unto this day time booms upon two bells
With drift of drizzling echoes in the mist,
For when your Spanish ships went down, you learned
That by whatever names they may be called,
Things beautiful and happy are foredoomed.
Your childish heart held more than childish woe
Not to be comforted till you should see
The Spanish fleet come sailing home from limbo,
And even fancy could not blur the knowledge
That they would never come, and that was ended.
There was a horror in the victory,

Something eternal left you at that moment
Confirmed apprentice to your master, Time.

Seize on another strand of memory
And follow. You were playing blind man's buff
With other children in a darkening room.
The bandage pressed so tight upon your eyes
That stars and flashes flickered to and fro.
You were bewildered as your playmates changed
To savage ambushes of touch and sound,
Brushing against you, pinching, plucking at you,
And muttering in far corners of the room.
You heard soft footsteps going away, and then
Nothing but silence. Were they gone? or hiding?
You waited a long while, grew slowly frightened,
Then cold with panic snatched the blindfold off
And stared into the void of a black room.
You were alone. Through the two open windows
Where the blue twilight glimmered, two bells clanged.
You whispered, " I must run into the hall."
Then with a voice that scarcely could be heard:
" Is anybody here? " " Of course, of course,
Turn up the gas. Darling, it's only a game;
Look, here's your rabbit. Here is Doctor Bun.
Now Doctor Bun, tell him it was a game;
They didn't mean it; everything's all right."

And so your patent of mortalilty
Was sealed, both by the double note of time
And the dark walls of space, which hedged you in
Henceforth from the wide reaches of the day.

You tell me you were born . . . where was it then?
I have forgotten. Follow deeper still
To a world blind with steam through which the sun
Glimmers uncertainly with bloodshot light.
There you stand in ooze up to your ankles,
And all around except for where the sea
Whimpers along the edges of the marsh
The jungle closes in with drip of leaves
And gurgle of hot mud where bubbles swell
With vapour, puff, collapse, and swell again.
A scaly head comes bulging through the muck
And stares with witless and unwinking eyes.
Then the ground heaves, a tremor quivers through it,
The fog sighs palely with a lightning flash,
Low thunder booms, and from the middle sky
The echo travels back in minor thirds.
There in that shadowless expanse you stand
While something horrible you can not name
Gathers along your spine. The fog thickens
And then the horror is upon you. Night.

O well to live above these memories,
Well for your reason in his upper sky

To shine through the clear air of fact, nor pierce
Too deep into the fog of nether worlds.
O well for you . . . but think not to forget
The savage birthplace I remember for you.
Look at the pliant skin which clothes your hands, —
Look closer. Ah, the lizard scales, the pores
Agape to breathe the hot steam of the marsh.
The jungle seethes, and lust with roving eyes
That shine through darkness, leaps upon despair
And mates with her. And when the wandering moon
Half-seen through never-lifting depth of fog
Has nine times closed her circle in the dawn
Despair brings forth the wonder-child of lust.
These were your parents in that early birthplace
And in the lowest marches of your mind
They prowl the jungle of the double thunder
Screaming against the filtered light of reason
As dogs behowl the moon, till reason's self,
Faint with the fumes from those primeval fens,
Swoons in the zenith. O desperate one,
Will you return to that dank world you left
Æons ago, or plunging boldly through it
Traverse yet farther to that other day
Which lies beyond it, where the unbroken light
Before the worlds were, brought you into being?
If in the short progression of this earth
You have thrown wide the doors of life and seen

The jungle creatures, shrunk to tiny vermin,
Scatter from sight among the mouldy walls,
And the vast trees, diminishing through ages,
Become the fronds of horsetail and of fern
You trample down on paths of afternoon,
You shall yet see all things that knew the jungle
Shrink, while the spirit grows till it behold
This burnt-out planet smaller than an ember
Whirling from sight along an autumn wind.

At dawn when you awake from your short sleep
And the poor dream of living that you had,
You shall arise and wash your heart with laughter
Under the trees beside the shadowed waters.
Come, snatch the blindfold off, and hush the bells
That ring against the Spanish fleets of dream,
Behold around the final headland steaming,
Vizcaya, Cristobal Colon, Oquendo,
Teresa, Pluton, Furor, — homeward bound.

II

Death

We come on leaden feet, we come with leaden
Tread along the haunted corridors
Through darkness void as in a dying brain
Where one by one the thoughts have flickered out.
The curves of our grey surplices flow soft
In every crevice of your memory,
And not an ingle of your mind or body
Eludes our still invasion. You shall hear
The fields whispering under the thin rain
Raw on autumnal earth though spring is here.
We will wring acid tears that bite the eyes
For someone dead whom you have never seen.
Hear how unending rain upon his grave
Seeps downward till it whimpers on his bones.
He loved the glow of fire upon his hands
That now lie splashed with mud beneath the rain, —
Think of him out there when you wake at midnight.

You never knew him, but we tell you, we
Whose office is to enlist the death-watch for him,
In him you weep the doom that is your own.
Look at your hands, the blue veins showing through,
Fantastically outlined against the fire,

The rain will sog the fingers like the petals
Which lie on the wet grass when spring is done.

You will remember Love, cry out to Love,
Who held your body close against the world,
You will remember how the arms of Love
Were round you in the little curtained room
Where the clock ticked. You will remember how
With every slash of rain against the window
When the wind wailed, she drew you ever closer
And pressed you down, so safe, so kind she was
And joyful in the secret gifts of love.
You will call out to her from underground
As children from their nightmares call for help:
Beloved, look! My body is so cold,
The earth seeps in on me and the cold rain;
Fling back the curtain, tell me this is a dream,
Wake me! deliver me! I am gagged with death.
She will not hear you, she will never come.

You did not know the dead man, so you say.
But you have known those who have followed him.
Think of them out there. What? so soon forgotten?
And of what merits, then, are you possessed
To ensure a longer dwelling in remembrance?
Think of each one in turn. Give them your name,
Think how they held their hands out to the fire

And glowed through every vein. They saw no end
To the anatomy of thought and sinew
Which made their universe, — themselves the universe;
They were important beings to themselves.

Count over all your friends, your loves, your children,
And say, I have been dead a year or two;
How fondly am I living through their lives?
Go through them slowly, one by one by one.
Your friends recall you once or twice a year
To try the idiom of tenderness
Wherein you are no more than is a title
Set to a poem perfect in itself.
Your loves dared not to think of you a while,
And then they merely did not think of you,
And when at last in the gay resurrection
Nature reserves for those who have not died
They looked into new eyes and love bewildered
Their mortal boughs with burgeoning again,
How should they ponder over the dead leaves,
How should they turn away from the clear look
Of favour in the eyes of life, to brood
On dim reproaches in the eyes of death
Sunk in their skull beneath the drenching rain?
Your children have inherited your wealth,
The most persuasive comforter of woe,
Or else, perhaps, your poverty, and they

Speak never of you, lest too bitterly.
O sooner than the earth recalls its own,
Before the flesh unfastens from the bone,
The memory of you buried in the heart
Of one still living softly falls apart.
Your face upturned against the earth and rain
Outlasts the image of it in his brain,
Your phantom tread on stairways of his thought
Falters, recedes, grows fainter, and is gone.
Even your senseless immortality
Of grass rots in the rain

But now you say
You hear your heart still ticking? You still live?
But listen closer, the beat fluctuates,
The arteries swell with uncertain pulse
And all within you, the corrupted highway
Of nerves and muscles, rutted and worn away
With traffic of your many joys and sorrows,
Grows lax in the foreboding of its end.

We come with leaden footsteps, we will wake
You under the midnight, we will wake you under
The midnight when the world has fallen away.
Life has receded from you like a tide,
Leaving the flats to view, where empty shells
Of dead experience echo the ebbing waves.

We will remember for you all your follies,
The bungled kiss, the passionate ineptness,
We will compute the garner of the years,
The eyes grown dim to colour, ears to sound,
Nostrils to perfume, every nerve gone slack
To untune the instrument on which you played
Such gallant music for your little while.
We come with leaden tread, we come on leaden
Feet; you shall go with us, you shall go
With us down to the deeper caves of midnight,
While the unending rain falls on the earth,
Drumming on roofs, on pavements, on the graves
Of men who loved the warmth upon their hands,
And sweet sensations in a little room.
Listen! your heart is growing fainter, Listen!
It leaps once and . . . Listen! Only the rain
On midnight fields from which no harvest comes.

III

Ecstasy

We are the glory-dancers, we will dance
You over the mountain, we will dance you over
The mountain, we will dance you over the sea.
Our feet will flash before you among the crags
Or dart along the seaways. You will say
The twinkle of sun is dazzling to my eyes.
— But listen! and you will hear the rainbow. Listen,
And you will hear us shout. Listen, and you,
Borne on that music, will slide sideways into
The air, your body itself will float in ether.
Perhaps you will say, I do not like this song;
It minds me of the swan who sings and dies,
Or of the swan who curses God and dies,
Or of the swan who sees Naples and dies.
Curses and sees, and dies. Or sings and dies.
— But lift out of the death. Lift with a song
Out of the death. Lift *with* the song of death!
Or perhaps you will say, be with me for this moment
Of ecstasy, and then begone, begone,
Lest I should see your face among the books
I read for my employment in the alley.
— Let us be tiger-hearted, let us be
Tiger-hearted, let us be suns of splendour,

Swift and sleek along the dewdrops of weeds
That scare the ploughman ploughing for lonely bread.

O coward, you have dreamed it! you have floated
Heavenward over the eyes of applauding friends.
Do you need a dream for flight? do you nead a dream
To launch into the air aslant with yielding?
Do you need the plaudits of your friends to fly?
Take life then as a dream, take us for friends,
For we invisible are nimbler still
Than you, though you traverse the centuries
Full thirty cubits down Egyptian mould.
For we are wingless, being ourselves the wings.
We will applaud you, we will seize the crowns
Of Ætna and Vesuvius to fling
Across your orbit. We will make you proud
Knowing ourselves profundities of pride
And dream beyond your Romes and Arcadies.
Beneath our eyes the iron cities rust,
And kings show meanly in grey films of dust
On which the housemaid writes her name; we are
The light between the telescope and star,
Out-riding years of light. We fling ourselves
Into the void while constellations sing.

Snow falls on snow till worlds are buried in snow,
Flowers on flowers till deserts are paths of sand,

And oceans, pools in a garden too large for the heartbeat
Of any except two lovers when you are one,
Of any except two lovers when all are one.
Look not for our footsteps in summer unless you are clever
In charting the path of the wind on the leaves. Perhaps
In winter the swirl of our merriment brushing the snow-
    drifts
Will give you a pattern. Perhaps if you swim undersea
You will find, even fainter than tracks from the fin of a
    minnow,
The figures our swift minuet will inscribe on the sand.

We are the glory-dancers. We dance glory
To you and to ourselves; our feet discharge
Long yellow flashes as of flint on steel
Between red Mars and white Aldebaran.
We are the glory, we are the dancers, you
Will dance with us, you will dance glory with us,
Over the mountain, over the ocean, over
The mountain, over the sea, beyond the mountain,
Beyond the mountain and the sea. Beyond.

IV

Love

As if with deep foreknowledge like the earth
Which murmurs spring before the spring is heard,
She slipped her hand in his and led him forth
Through secret ways that opened on a hill
Where the wind rippling up the grass sent waves
Of green to lose themselves against the sky
And downward tumbled glittering waters, shouting
Of waterfalls and oceans yet to come.
The lovers wandered, neither daring now
One word of what their hearts were clamouring,
Until, his arm through hers, he turned her toward him
And face to face they trembled in the sunlight.

He whispered, " Are the eyes that dreamed so long
Of love afraid of love? " " They are not afraid,"
She answered, " they are dazzled with the sun."
" Let us throw off our dreams then; let us cast
Our fears away," he said, " as we threw off
Our garments; let us, naked of our past,
Climb up the flowery slope. Be now your heart
My heart, the quickening beat in both the song
Of lovers climbing hills in early morning.
Your breath that slumbered for the thousand years

And mine that battled with the wind are mingled
In the strong gasp of happiness prevailing
Yet for a swifter pulse and richer blood
To sweep through every vein; O may this hill
Not end, O may we never reach the crest
But like a bird that out of sight and hearing
Spirals upward in the ecstasy
Of death, mount to the sun. . . . O my Beloved,
Are you afraid? " " No, not afraid, not now.
Let us a while lie here in the long grass
And as our heartbeats slow to calmer pace
Still be their measure one. I fear only
That I should sleep and wake to find you gone,
Sleep for a thousand years, and find you gone.
Or else that death should come on one of us;
No, I am not afraid of love," she said.
He lifted up his hand and pointed far
Where range on range the blue hills fell away.
" Those lie before us, or before our children,
And we have passed beyond the fear of death
Who have passed beyond the fear of love. O never
Shall death come near us now. I can not tell you
Whether we still are on the whirling earth
Or far beyond it, unaware immortals;
I can not tell you whether we shall always,
You with your name and I with mine, go forth
To climb the hills before the dew has left them.

But if not we, our children; and if not
This love of ours, the same love born in them.
What more of everlastingness could gods
Ask than to behold their flesh renewed
In fairer bodies, and their old desires
Flowering from greener stems that are their own?
Happy were I to be as now for ever,
But change is on the world and if we change
We shall but leave this to our fairer selves, —
The rest is but a love of little names."
But as he spoke she turned away from him
And gazed far down the slope whence they had come,
Back to the sleeping palace, and beyond it
The forest wrapped in fog, whence mournfully
Sounded the echoes of two bells. He smiled
Seeing she had not heard him, and was silent
Until a darker thought swam over him
Like clouds across the sunlight, and he shuddered.
"I seemed to hear . . . was it two bells I heard?
Was it the slash of rain against the window
Before we died? Forgive me, I am strange
To credit happiness. I thought you dead
And would have gathered up the pitiful dust
That was your body, held it in my hand,
And breathing on it, blown my life away
For east or west to gather, autumn or spring.
I would have shed my years to stand beside you

Leafless, shed my hearing and my sight,
My thoughts, since you were no more to be heard
Or seen nor thought of; yes, and before that
I can remember weariness of worship
In those few days of our companionship
When I consumed you utterly, and still
With the last atom of your excellence
Yearned for you more. I would have lost myself
Wholly in you, held nothing back, I would
Have been you only, though at last your dust
Was little on my palm." "Let death go by,"
She answered, " in the wind rustling the leaves,
Depart without departure, blow away
And still blow on, only its music lingering."
Then artfully and timidly, she asked him,
" During my thousand years of sleep where were you
Besides the broken dream I had of you?
I saw the sunlight chequered through the trellis
And would have asked that life go on for ever
With music and with toys and make-believe.
But suddenly I slept. Where were you then
Through all that pausing summer afternoon?
— Tell me, for I am jealous of the past."
" I too might well have slept. There is no story
Which is not you, Beloved. What befell me
Might befall any man. Perhaps I learned
More of deceit than most because I trusted

All men and women more than most. My friends
Betrayed me, women lied to me; and once
I swung my sword against reputed foes
Who when the fog of battle cleared away
Whispered with dying lips my brother's name."
" Peace, that is over. Tears for that dead sorrow
Would kill the living joy. Those countries now
Are less than dreams and the lost dreamers there
Have all forgotten you. Your friends remembered
Your name a while; your loves dared not remember,
But all are one now in forgetting you."
He laughed, " That was a dread I had at midnight,
Now it is like a cup of sunny wine
To lips that shuddered, thinking it of hemlock.
So long, so bitter, the weeping upon earth,
So short the hours under the drunken arbour
Where body and body search the plangent nerves
And find no answer to their loud demanding.
All have we done that mortal things can do,
We have been born, been loved, been slain and buried,
And still unsatisfied because our beauty
Is greater than we gave or could be taken,
We have done nothing, all has worked upon us,
Loved us too much and left us after love
In bondage of inaction. Not until
I put behind me the false loves which are
But vanity that feeds on adoration,

Not till I scattered them, their flatteries
Still mouthing on the air, and sought you out
Could I be sure that death and you were parted,
That dust was not a rival, that I could
Ride back and back through calendars of doubt
And find you in the end as in the beginning."

She said again, " These thousand years, where were you?
Tell me, for I am jealous of your past."
" Must I remember? there are planes of music
Which would bring back without an absent tinge
The little curtained room, the log fire burning,
And the old love, but all these moments knew
Themselves foredoomed, seeing within the crystal
Of their own ecstasy the grey forms gathering,
Cowled, with averted gaze, because their joy
Was but a song beleaguered by the silence.
There were no loves which were not you, Beloved.
Till now when I am healed, there was no time
I did not seek you to fulfill the dream
You had during your long sleep and forgot.
Before the world was; yes, before the thought
Of any world had sundered the great light
Into the rainbow, then we were together
And now we are together once again.
That is enough, O trust me! though you saw
Me prowling jungles of despair and lust

To mate with monstrous loves within my thought.
And I am here as one who finds redemption
Out of his earnings in another world."
" Shall I confess," she whispered, " that I dreamed
Without forgetfulness? But of that dream
I can not tell you all, nor any woman
Tell to any man. I saw you shaping
My image through so many others, saw them
The hateful and the beautiful, myself
In many forms adroit to do your pleasure
According to your will. For you I was
Savage and desperate under the wan moon,
I was the handmaid of your self-esteem
Or the deliverer from fear. I slept
Not peacefully who dreamed so many shames.
I could not waken to this happiness
Till you were weary of my counterfeits
And sought me out and bade me rise, myself,
None other, so made perfect in your love."

So faded the two lovers up the hillside,
And yet when they had seemed for ever vanished
They glimmered in the half-light as they passed
Over the fields between the scattered copses.
And when the veering wind blew straight across
From hill to hill, their voices floated back,
A murmured phrase, sometimes a gust of laughter.

And as the evening star rose clear before them
They reached the summit of the second hill,
Where lifted to a momentary glory
They stood against the sky, and so were gone.

INDEX OF FIRST LINES

Index of First Lines

A NOTE ON THE TYPE
IN WHICH THIS BOOK IS SET

This book is printed in *Estienne,* a linotype face designed by George W. Jones, the eminent English printer, and named in honour of the Estienne family. Henri Estienne (died 1520), a descendant of a Provençal noble family, came to Paris in 1502 and set up a printing establishment there. After his death his widow married his foreman, Simon de Colines, who carried on the business until 1526, when it passed into the possession of Robert Estienne (1503–59), Henri's second son, who had been his step-father's assistant. In 1539 Robert was appointed king's printer by Francis I. As the result of disputes with the Faculty of Theology he moved to Geneva in 1551, where he set up a new printing establishment. His younger brother, Charles Estienne (*c.* 1504–64), took over the Paris establishment in 1551 and was appointed king's printer. Robert's son Henri Estienne (1531–98), a learned scholar, inherited the printing house at Geneva. Several disputes with the consistory inclined him to travel extensively in his later years. Later descendants continued the family tradition for scholarship and fine printing.

THE COMPOSITION, PRINTING, AND BINDING ARE BY *The Plimpton Press,* NORWOOD, MASS. THE PAPER IS MADE BY *S. D. Warren Co.,* BOSTON.

MAR 1 4 1953